TECHNICAL REPORT

Network-Based Operations for the Swedish Defence Forces

An Assessment Methodology

WALTER PERRY, JOHN GORDON IV,
MICHAEL BOITO, GINA KINGSTON

TR-119-FOI

June 2004

Prepared for the Swedish Defence Research Agency

Approved for public release; distribution unlimited

RAND EUROPE

The research described in this report was prepared for the Swedish Defence Research Agency.

Library of Congress Cataloging-in-Publication Data

Network-based operations for the Swedish defence forces : an assessment methodology /
  Walter Perry ... [et al.].
      p. cm.
    "TR-119."
    Includes bibliographical references.
    ISBN 0-8330-3539-8 (pbk. : alk. paper)
      1. Sweden—Armed Forces—Organization. 2. Unified operations (Military science)
  3. Sweden—Defenses. 4. Sweden—Military policy. I. Perry, Walt L.

UA790.N397 2004
355.3'09485—dc22

2003025742

The RAND Corporation is a nonprofit research organization providing objective analysis and effective solutions that address the challenges facing the public and private sectors around the world. RAND's publications do not necessarily reflect the opinions of its research clients and sponsors.

RAND® is a registered trademark.

Published 2004 by the RAND Corporation
1700 Main Street, P.O. Box 2138, Santa Monica, CA 90407-2138
1200 South Hayes Street, Arlington, VA 22202-5050
201 North Craig Street, Suite 202, Pittsburgh, PA 15213-1516
RAND URL: http://www.rand.org/
To order RAND documents or to obtain additional information, contact
Distribution Services: Telephone: (310) 451-7002;
Fax: (310) 451-6915; Email: order@rand.org

Preface

The Swedish government is undertaking efforts to reorient Swedish Defence Forces from defence against invasion to operational defence—a significant change in the way Sweden is willing to employ the country's armed forces. Because operational defence includes expeditionary operations with coalition partners, a decision was made to move toward a fully networked force that is capable of participating with other nations—including the United States—in international military operations.

The Swedish Defence Research Agency (FOI) asked the RAND Corporation to develop a methodology to assess alternative network structures and operational concepts to support the Swedish Defence Forces' transition to a fully network-based force. This report outlines a methodology aimed at assessing the costs and benefits of architectures for network-based operations.

This research was sponsored by the Swedish Defence Research Agency and conducted within RAND Europe and the International Security and Defense Policy Center of RAND's National Security Research Division (NSRD), which conducts research for the U.S. Department of Defense, allied foreign governments, the intelligence community, and foundations.

For more information on RAND's International Security and Defense Policy Center, contact the Director, Jim Dobbins. He can be reached by e-mail at James_Dobbins@rand.org; by phone at 703-413-1100, extension 5134; or by mail at RAND Corporation, 1200 South Hayes Street, Arlington, VA 22202-5050. More information about the RAND Corporation is available at www.rand.org.

Contents

Figures

Tables

Summary

Network-centric warfare (NCW), or network-based warfare, is generally thought
to be "an information superiority enabled concept of operations that generates
increased combat power through the networking of sensors, decision makers and
shooters, to achieve shared awareness, increased speed of command, higher
tempo of operations, greater lethality, increased survivability, and a degree of
self-synchronization" (Alberts et al., 2002, p. 2). In contrast to network-based
operations or warfare, traditional warfare is considered to be *platform-centric*.
The difference between the two is that each weapon system in platform-centric
warfare acts independently, so that one must mass force to mass combat
effectiveness, whereas, in network-centric warfare, effects are massed rather than
forces. For this reason, network-based operations are attractive to the Swedish
Defence Forces.

A structural or logical model for network-based operations has emerged. Its
fundamental requirement is a high-performance information network that
provides the capacity for computing and communications among entities
participating in a given operation. This is what we refer to as the *network
infrastructure*.

An effort is under way to complete Sweden's military modernisation effort by
2015, focusing on warfare in the 2025 time frame. An early product of this effort,
scheduled for completion in 2005, is to be an operational network design. The
design will include, among other things, an architecture, a communications
infrastructure, and a sensor management plan. The tools to assess the cost and
effectiveness of the design must be in place early to assist in that process. The
Swedish Defence Research Agency (FOI) is tasked with developing a
methodology to identify the costs and benefits of alternative network structures.

Research Objective

The primary objective of this research is to develop a general methodology that
can be used to assess the costs of performing a wide range of military functions
using alternative network structures: in essence, to define an analytic process.
Although we do not address the benefits directly, we address them indirectly
through the requirements for an operational network. We recognise that the
Swedish military will also require a more direct assessment of the benefits.

This project comprises two basic tasks: (1) Identify the operational functions to be served by a comprehensive network-based defence structure and (2) identify support activities needed to perform these functions and recommend an approach for assessing their costs, as well as the costs of the network infrastructure and the operational infrastructure. The application of the recommended approach to an operational function and illustrative network infrastructures is left for future work.

Sweden's Emerging Defence Policy Options

The 1999 Swedish policy paper *The New Defence—prepared for the next millennium* highlights the magnitude of the changes in international relations that have taken place in recent years. The report states:

> The Swedish defence system is about to undergo necessary renewal and modernization. The reason for this is the security situation in the world at large. We can now create a modern, flexible and versatile defence on the basis of national service. The units and systems that will be needed in the future should be capable of being utilized for both the defence of Sweden and participation in international operations.

The government envisions that, in 2004, important decisions will be made that will guide the future orientation and structure of the Swedish armed forces. Three of the four options under consideration place considerable emphasis on coalition military operations outside Sweden. The decisions will provide guidance to the armed forces on the direction they are to take in the next 10 to 15 years.

Operational Functions

Among the problems facing system architects and analysts are (1) identifying the full spectrum of military operations to be conducted in a network-based structure and (2) understanding just how such operations will be performed and what level of network-based support the operations will require. The operational functions supported by the network are those associated with the selected option for the Swedish Defence Force's future structure. In any case, the functions will have full-spectrum requirements, which fall into four broad categories:

Combat Operations: Functions directly related to combat operations, such as air and missile defense, and joint command and control.

Peacetime Operations: Other functions, such as supply and personnel management, are more applicable to normal peacetime operations.

Interagency Operations: Still other functions relate to interagency operations, for which the military has to exchange information and data with other government departments.

Noncombat Coalition Operations: These include functions such as humanitarian assistance operations and assistance to local civil authorities.

Prioritisation

Given the costs and technological challenges associated with creating a large-scale military network, there is a need to prioritise the effort. The 2004 defence decision should provide important guidance for Swedish military planners and technologists, who can then prioritise which aspects of a military network can receive immediate attention. For example, if it is determined that homeland defence will still be emphasised, then a function such as air and missile defence would probably receive high priority. If, on the other hand, international operations are to be emphasised, other aspects of a military network, such as a joint command system with the ability to interface with selected nations that are likely coalition partners, would assume greater priority in terms of resources.

Emerging U.S. Vision

From the dawn of organised conflict, military strategists have used communications and information to beat the enemy. The ancient Greeks dispatched runners over long distances to deliver military messages. European infantries used drummers to communicate common battle orders to soldiers fighting together who did not speak the same language. Network-centric warfare sprang from a need, dramatised in World War II and Vietnam, to use information technology to create a more lethal fighting force, as well as to avoid casualties from friendly fire. Although currently most widely used within the U.S. Navy, where it was first developed, NCW is emerging as a key operational concept to support the U.S. military's force transformation. The nature of NCW is such that large weapon systems, such as ships, can take advantage of its benefits more readily than can the more dispersed Army formations.

Methodology

The methodology proposed in this report assumes that the operational functions have been prioritised and networks have been proposed to support theoperational functions. The operational functions are then grouped intointeraction categories according to their requirements. These categories support the identification of common subnetworks and of analogous systems or components in the cost-estimation process.

Categories of Interaction

Although it may be a theoretical ideal to have all military functions available on a single federated network that all military users can access, the reality is that there will be a stratification of users according to their need to have access to the data, their function, hardware and software costs, and security concerns. In most cases, the subnetwork will dictate access requirements. We refer to this stratification of users as the *categories of network interaction.*

The categories are distinguished in three ways: the degree of access required, including both the number of participants in the operational function and the variety of data required; the security requirements; and the timeliness, or time criticality, of the information needed to support the operational function. Each of the operational functions falls into one of the four categories of network interaction illustrated in Figure S.1.

Category 1—Specialised Interaction. In this category, the requirements are not as extreme as for those of the categories that follow. The requirements for access to information vary with participants' roles and the structure of the supporting subnetwork. The requirement for near-real-time access to information varies by participant. And although some security may be required, it is not a driving factor. The requirements for access, timeliness, and security may each range from medium to low, requirements that cover a wide range of networks, many of them not suitable for defence needs. For example, as the level of access, timeliness, and security approaches zero, the need for any form of network disappears.

Category 2—Ubiquitous Interaction. Functions that require this degree of network accessibility generally affect large numbers of organisations—for example, subnetworks that support personnel management activities, payroll, and supply functions, along with certain joint operations requiring several units from all services. In general, the several participants in the supported activity

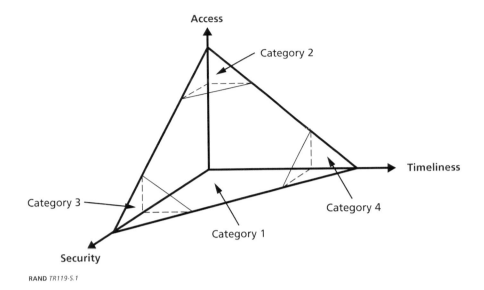

RAND *TR119-S.1*

Figure S.1—Interaction Categories

will require similar access to data and information on all aspects of the operation available on the federated network.

Category 3—Secure Interaction. Several operational functions require that both operations and information be secure, placing unique demands on the network for interactions among participants and the information exchanged to be secured both physically and electronically. Most intelligence operations, covert activities, and Special Forces operations are of this nature.

Category 4—Real-Time Interaction. Operations requiring this level of support are usually extremely time-sensitive combat actions that require that very few participants have access to critical real-time data and are able to share that data among all participants, even when network connections and nodes have failed. They are highly restrictive (few participants), intense operations, such as cruise and ballistic missile defence.

Deciding on an Interaction Category

One of the early tasks in assessing the costs and benefits of network-based operations is determining the category of network interaction each operational function requires. To make this task easier, it is helpful to establish measures that can assess the broad interaction requirements needed to support each operational function. The degree of interaction available from the federated network is clearly a function of the structure of the underlying information network available; therefore, the measures selected are designed to assess the federated network's ability to supply the full range of information services, on demand, to the entities participating in operational functions. These measures are defined in Chapter 3. In Table S.1, the measures that are used to determine which category an operation's function falls into are listed on the left; the categories of interaction are shown along the top.

Network requirements can be determined from the categorisation of the operational functions. The network architectures that will support those functions can be assessed from the network requirements directly, and the benefits of network-based operations can be assessed indirectly. The method used to analyse the architecture will depend on the requirements and the novelty of the architecture.[1] The categories also group similar networks for costing.

Table S.1

Determining Interaction-Category Thresholds

Measure	Category 1 Specialised	Category 2 Ubiquitous	Category 3 Secure	Category 4 Real-Time
Intensity	Medium	High	Medium	Low
Capacity	Medium	High	Medium	Low
Richness	Medium	High	Medium	Low
Reach	Medium	High	Low	Low
Monitoring	Medium	Low	High	High
Robustness	Medium	Low	High	High
Security	Medium	Low	High	Medium
Timeliness	Medium	Low	Medium	High

Illustrative Operational Functions

In theory, all relevant information needed to support operations is available for users to access in support of all operational functions. Under ideal circumstances, all participants in the network could gain access to and use any function in the network. In reality, the number of users for a particular function will be limited according to need-to-know, cost constraints, and other considerations.

---

[1] Assessment approaches are not discussed in detail; however, they may include analysis of both the network and the network components, using simulation, throughput-analysis tools, or comparison with existing networks or components.

The Swedish military should consider what operational functions it requires for inclusion in a network or federation of networks. Of the several operational functions that could be included in a network, three have been singled out for more detailed analysis: air and missile defence, joint air-land-sea battle command, and joint targeting. Examples of other operational functions that could be included in a Swedish military network include disaster relief, mass casualty response, supply management, and training status of individuals and units.

An additional important consideration for Sweden is the degree of international interoperability that should be included in its military networks. With emphasis being placed on multinational operations, the Swedish military must consider the degree to which its military networks should be interoperable with similar systems being developed by other nations.

Costing

Although our objective here is not to actually assess the costs associated with performing the operational functions in a network-based structure, we suggest a *general methodology* that can be applied to any operational function executed within any network-based structure. For a general methodology, we identify cost categories that encompass the network itself; its development, management, and maintenance; and the possible costs associated with performing operational functions in a network-based environment.

The following is a summary of cost-estimating practices, followed by a broad range of general approaches available to estimate network-based operations for Swedish Defence Forces. Next, we consider the lessons learned from the U.S. Navy's Cooperative Engagement Capability (CEC).[2] We conclude with a suggested methodology for estimating the cost of network-based operations in the Swedish Defence Forces.

Cost-Estimating Approaches

There are three basic approaches to cost estimating: bottom-up, analogy, and parametric. The following paragraphs provide an overview of the three approaches and their advantages and disadvantages.

---

[2] The CEC system links U.S. Navy ships and aircraft operating in a particular area into a single, integrated, air-defence network, in which radar data collected by each platform are transmitted on a real-time (i.e., instantaneous) basis to the other units in the network.

Bottom-Up: The bottom-up approach relies on detailed engineering analysis and calculation to estimate costs. Details the analyst needs are design and configuration information for all parts of the system being estimated, including material, equipment, and labour. The detailed design and cost estimate has the advantages of addressing many issues so that the effect of each issue is well understood.

Analogy: With the analogy approach, an analyst selects a similar or related system and makes adjustments for differences. This approach works well for derivative systems or evolutionary improvements to existing systems. Its main advantage over the bottom-up approach is that only the changes or differences must be estimated, which saves time and expense. However, a good starting baseline must exist for this method to be applied. For radical changes or new technologies, the bottom-up approach is more appropriate.

Parametric: A third approach uses parametric methods to forecast outcomes. *Parametric methods* attempt to explain cost as a function of other physical or technical characteristics, such as software lines of code, data throughput, and size or weight. This approach has as its principal advantage that its application is straightforward once the basic relationship has been defined. Unlike the first two approaches, a detailed conceptual design is not necessary to apply the method, although a method of determining the relevant input characteristics is required. Another, more subtle, advantage of parametric relationships generated using regression analysis is that one can also generate information on uncertainty of the forecasted value. In other words, one obtains a result of $y \pm e$, where e is related to the error terms of the regression. This uncertainty value can be just as informative as the predicted value.

A Methodology for Estimating Costs of Network-Based Operations

Assessing the costs and benefits of converting to a network-based defence structure requires a sound methodology that can help analysts to objectively compare alternative structures. The problem is to identify all costs and to adopt an accepted costing method to apply to each. The costs associated with implementing network-based operations derive from two broad categories: those associated with the network infrastructure and those associated with the operational functions to be supported by the network. The appropriate cost methodology should be able to estimate the costs of different networks that perform different operations at different support levels so that decisionmakers will have an idea of what kind and how many networks they can afford. The methodology should also be capable of comparing the cost of performing a given operation without a network with the cost of performing the operation in a network, thus allowing for a comparison of costs and benefits of a network for each operation.

Estimating Network Infrastructure Costs. The methodology to estimate network infrastructure costs requires that specific operational functions and networks have been selected for costing.

The first step in the methodology is to define an appropriate cost-element structure for the network. Network infrastructure (information network) costs include the investment costs of exploring and defining the network concept; costs of developing the system, including system design and specification, software development, and test and evaluation; and the costs of procuring and deploying facilities, hardware, and software. Network infrastructure costs will also include ongoing costs to operate and maintain the network and are generally driven by the costs of personnel and software maintenance.

There is no set or prescribed answer to the question: What is the appropriate level at which to define a cost-element structure and estimate costs? At the planning stage, when little detailed information is available about the system, it may not be possible to estimate at an expanded level of detail. Similarly, when detailed information on analogous systems is not available, it may not be possible to estimate in great detail. Yet, if the system to be estimated is very similar to an analogous system, it may be sufficient to estimate without much detail by drawing on the significant similarities.

However, it may be necessary to estimate at a detailed level when the system to be estimated is unique, and the estimator must look at many small components of the system for which cost methodologies are available to build up to the cost of the total system. Finally, when high resolution is required, and sufficient data, time, and money are available, a more detailed estimate may be appropriate.

The second step is to determine the interaction category appropriate for the selected operational functions. This means applying the measures and metrics described in Chapter 3.

The third step in the methodology is to link the capabilities and metrics of the network to elements of the infrastructure cost. The use of the metrics for assessing categories of interaction can assist in determining at least ordinal levels of cost differences for each cost element. Linking the capabilities and metrics of the network to the cost element then guides the choice of an appropriate estimating methodology, the next step.

The fourth step is to choose an appropriate cost-estimation methodology. Ideally, we would like to link each cost element with its capabilities and metrics and select a cost-estimating methodology that is sensitive to the key metrics. We may use analogies to other elements in the same interaction category, or perhaps a parametric cost-estimating relationship that used the metrics as inputs, or to formulate new cost-estimation relationships between metrics of the network and estimated costs.

Difficulties in Estimating Software-Intensive Systems. One of the most difficult areas of network infrastructure to cost is the software. Software-intensive systems have proven notoriously difficult to estimate in the United States. Many U.S. weapon systems have experienced cost growth and schedule delays because of problems in software development, which include frequent changes by the user, overlooked tasks, lack of coordination among functions during development, and poor estimating methodologies.

Methodology for Estimating Network Operations Costs. The cost methodology must also assess the costs of performing the military operation in terms of personnel, equipment, and consumable items, such as fuel or repair items. For example, it is conceivable that additional personnel would be required to interpret or use the additional information a network provides for a given operation. It is just as conceivable that fewer personnel would be required to synthesise or process data in a networked operation, if the network did the processing. It is also conceivable that networking will allow some participants in the network to have fewer sensors of their own because they benefit from the information provided by the entire network. In these ways, networking would reduce some equipment costs. In any event, the cost methodology should assess how the network will change the way an operation will be performed and estimate the resulting differences in personnel, equipment, and other relevant costs.

Identifying which operations are affordable to network and which operations have the highest ratio of benefits to costs, when the cost methodology is combined with a methodology for assessing benefits, provides decisionmakers the information they will need.

Conclusions

Developing a common reference for discussing network-based operations will be important as the Swedish military moves increasingly in the direction of this new way of commanding, controlling, and executing military operations.

The operational functions we discuss are examples of what could be included in a series of federated military networks. Some functions would have applicability in normal peacetime operations as well as during an actual military operation. Other functions are more directly related to actual operations. The major defence policy decisions that Sweden will make in the coming years will help guide the prioritisation of these functions. Fiscal and technology realities will mean that networking will gradually enter the Swedish military; therefore, priority should be given to first introducing functions that relate to the types of operations the Swedish military is most likely to undertake.

We devoted considerable attention to the costing of military networks—a still-imprecise art, much less a science. Since the concept of network-based operations is still being introduced into the more technologically advanced militaries of the world, there are few lessons and past experiences that provide guidance on how to approach costing of new systems. The report provides insights on what are likely to be major cost drivers in military networks, one of the most critical, and most difficult to predict, being software development. Early definition of requirements can help in this area. Since the Swedish military is still developing its concepts of network-based operations, it is still too early to predict with any accuracy the eventual costs of a network. However, those involved in the networking effort in Sweden should be aware of the major issues associated with network development costs, which we have highlighted in this report.

A next step is to apply the approach to an operational function and illustrative network infrastructures.

Acknowledgments

The authors wish to express their gratitude to several individuals who provided guidance and assistance to the project. At Sweden's FOI, we wish to thank Christian Carling of the Division of Defence Analysis' Department of Command and Control Studies and Martin Hamrin of the Division of Defence Analysis' Department of Military Operational Research. Meeting with them greatly added to our understanding of the future direction of the Swedish Armed Forces in general and Sweden's military networking ideas in particular. At Sweden's Defence Acquisition Agency, FMV, the actual sponsor of the work, we wish to thank Goran Skogsberg from the Information and Communications group. His participation in the effort was of great benefit to the study team. At RAND Corporation, Robin Davis served as the final organiser of the report and ensured that the product was properly formatted and prepared.

Glossary

AAW	Anti–Air Warfare
ALO	Air Liaison Officers
AWACS	Advanced Warning Aircraft Control System
C4ISR	Command and Control, Communications, Computing, Intelligence, Surveillance, and Reconnaissance.
CEC	Cooperative Engagement Capability: A network developed by the U.S. Navy that fuses information on air defence from airborne and ship sensors into a single, integrated picture of fire-control quality
CER	Cost Estimating Relationship
CES	Cost Estimating System
DFSP	Common Foreign and Security Policy
Combined operations	Operations with coalition forces
Directed information flow	A one-way flow of information from one node to another and not vice versa.
EDS	Electronic Data Systems
Engagement-decision-shooter grid	A dynamic, need-based network that makes use of sensors and operational elements in the information grid to conduct the action required for a given operational function.
ESDP	European Security and Defence Policy
EU	European Union
FMV	Defence Acquisition Agency [Sweden]
FOI	Defence Research Agency [Sweden]
FORCEnet	A nascent NCW system designed to link sensors, networks, decision aids, weapons, and supporting systems into a single system.
Force synchronisation	The purposeful arrangement of force elements and actions in time and space.
Fusion	The process of combining information from multiple sources to generate new, improved, or standardised information.
GCCS	Global Command and Control System (U.S.)

GIG	U.S. Global Information Grid
GMTI	Ground Mobile Target Indicator
HF	High-frequency
Homeland Defence	Operations conducted on home soil. The home nation may be supported by other nations.
HTML	Hypertext Markup Language; information format type.
Information network grid	The infrastructure to receive, process, transport, store, and protect information for the joint and combined service
International Operations	Operations conducted on foreign soil, usually as part of an international coalition. Sweden's envisaged international operations are focused on peacekeeping, peace building, and/or peace enforcement.
Interoperability	The ability of alliance forces and, when appropriate, forces of partner and other nations to train, exercise, and operate together in the execution of assigned missions and tasks.
JSTARS	Joint Surveillance Targeting and Attack Radar System
Logical connectivity	Connectivity between nodes that is required to support an operational function and that is realised by one or more physical connections. The physical connections represent a certain hierarchy, or logic, in that two nodes are logically connected if they can talk to each other, even if the physical connectivity consists of dozens of hops.
Measures	Standards for comparison.
Mega centre	A large, central location from which network operations are managed.
Metrics	Mathematical expressions that evaluate both the relative effect of alternatives and the degree to which one alternative is better or worse than another.
NCO	Network-centric operations
NCW	Network-centric warfare: a set of warfighting concepts designed to create and leverage information.
Network	A group of nodes and their connections. The physical network consists of nodes and their physical connection. The logical network consists of nodes and their hierarchical, or logical, connections.
OFT	Office of Force Transformation
Operational function	All of the activities the Swedish Defence Forces must perform in support of the four main military tasks: defending against armed attacks; upholding territorial integrity; contributing to international peace and

	security; and strengthening Swedish society in the event of severe peacetime emergencies.
Peace Enforcement	Operations to keep or build peace in which the use of force is permissible.
Peacekeeping and Peace Building	Operations to keep or build peace without the use of force.
PfP	Partnership for Peace
Physical connectivity	Direct connectivity between nodes that is manifest in the physical environment—for example, the direct connection of nodes in a network by wires, cables, electromagnetic radiation, or other means.
SAM	Surface-to-Air Missile
Sensor network grid	A need-based network—for example, the CED—that makes use of sensors in the information grid that are pertinent to a given operational function
SLOC	Source lines of code
UHF	Ultra-high frequency
VMF	Vector Markup Language; information format type.
WEU	West European Union
XML	Extensible Markup Language; information format type.

1. Introduction

The Swedish Defence system is in the early stages of a "renewal and modernization" programme in response to global changes in the political-military climate. Central to this renewal is an increased effort to contribute both diplomatically and militarily to the collective security of Europe—a shift in Sweden's defence posture from one of homeland defence to one of ensuring European security.[1] This more flexible defence policy is compelled by the uncertain international climate following the end of the Cold War. The Swedish Government Bill 1999/2000 (Swedish Ministry of Defence, 2001a) states explicitly that:

> It is not possible . . . to lock the defence system into a single view of future developments. Instead we must seek to build up an adaptation capability in which uncertainty about the future is an important starting point.

To implement this policy, Swedish Defence Forces have committed to network-based operations across the full spectrum of its military tasks: defending against armed attacks; upholding territorial integrity; contributing to international peace and security; and strengthening Swedish society in the event of severe peacetime emergencies. Network-centric, or network-based, operations are generally thought to be "an information superiority enabled concept of operations that generates increased combat power through the networking of sensors, decision makers and shooters, to achieve shared awareness, increased survivability, and a degree of self-synchronization" (Alberts et al., 2002, p. 2).

The decision to adopt a network-based operating structure was partially based on a belief that such a structure is the most efficient way to deliver military effects with limited resources.

Objective

The Swedish Defence Research Agency (FOI) is tasked with developing alternative military futures in support of the Swedish Armed Forces. The goal is to provide input to Sweden's Department of Defence decision in 2004. An

---

[1] In the Budget Bill 2002 Fact Sheet (Swedish Ministry of Defence, 2001b), this change was expressed as a "reorientation from defence against invasion to operational defence."

important task in this process is to identify the costs and benefits of network structures needed to support the alternative military futures.

An effort is under way to complete the modernisation effort by 2015, focusing on warfare in the 2025 time frame. An early product of this effort is to be an operational network design, which is scheduled for completion in 2005. It will include, among other things, an architecture, a communications infrastructure, and a sensor management plan. The tools to assess the cost and effectiveness of the design must be in place early to assist in that process.

The primary objective of this work is to develop a general methodology—an analytic process—that can be used to assess the costs of performing a wide range of military functions using alternative network structures. Although we do not address the benefits directly, we recognise that benefits are an important aspect of the methodology. Previous RAND research is available that addresses the assessment of network performance in support of military operations and will be used as a source during implementation of this methodology (Perry et al., unpublished; Perry et al., 2001).

We view this project as consisting of two basic tasks: (1) Identify the operational functions to be served by a comprehensive network-based defence structure and (2) identify support activities needed to perform these functions and recommend an approach for assessing their cost as well as the costs of the network infrastructure and the operational infrastructure.

Operational Functions

By *operational functions,* we mean all of the activities the Swedish Defence Forces must perform in support of the four main military tasks mentioned above, ranging from those associated with peacetime emergencies, foreign and domestic, to those associated with defending Sweden against an armed attack. Implicit in this catalogue is a prioritisation based on the distribution of resources that will be devoted to support to international operations, domestic defence, and contingencies as indicated in the Swedish Armed Forces long-range planning (personal communication, 2002).

Costing

The objective of this report is not to actually assess the costs associated with performing the operational functions in a network-based structure. Rather, it is to suggest a *general methodology* that can be applied to any operational function executed within any network-based structure. This means identifying cost categories that encompass the network itself; its development, management, and maintenance; and performing operational functions in a network-based environment.

This project is part of a comprehensive effort to examine all aspects of network-based operations so that appropriate network assessment tools can be recommended. The results of this project will be used to guide development of such a network.

Recent Defence Policy Changes in Sweden

On May 9, 1994, Sweden signed NATO's Partnership for Peace (PfP) (programme), which aims "to promote transparency in national defence planning and military budgeting and the democratic control of national armed forces, as well as to develop the capacity for joint action between forces from Partner countries and those of NATO member countries, for example, in peacekeeping or disaster-response operations" (NATO, 2002).[2] Sweden entered the European Union (EU) in 1995; entry included a commitment to the Common Foreign and Security Policy (CFSP). Today, Sweden has committed military forces for EU-sponsored peace operations of the type envisioned in the Petersberg Tasks.[3] By the middle of this first decade of the 21st century, Sweden will be prepared to commit forces for crisis management and combat operations under the auspices of the European Union. This commitment is consistent with the role of Swedish forces that have been deployed to peace support operations in the Balkans in reinforced battalion strength since the early 1990s. In February 2002, Sweden reached important agreements for increased defence industrial cooperation with the United States ("Sweden, U.S. in Trade Deal," 2002, p. 1). Sweden also deployed over 1,500 military personnel to participate in NATO's Combined Endeavour 2002 exercise.[4]

---

[2] See also the list of signatures and additional documentation at http://www.nato.int/pfp/pfp.htm.

[3] The *Petersberg Tasks* refer to the peace operations missions that the European Union has decided are the appropriate military missions for the initial EU military force. The West European Union (WEU) Ministerial Council agreed on these tasks in June 1992. They include humanitarian rescue, peacekeeping, and tasks of combat forces in crisis management, including peacemaking. See European Union (1992).

[4] "The basic aims of PfP are to promote transparency in national defence planning and military budgeting and the democratic control of national armed forces, as well as to develop the capacity for joint action between forces from Partner countries and those of NATO member countries, for example, in peacekeeping or disaster-response operations."

Defence Decision 2004

The 1999 Swedish Ministry of Defence policy paper *The New Defence—prepared for the next millennium* highlights the magnitude of the changes that have taken place in recent years. The report states on page 3 that

> The Swedish defence system is about to undergo necessary renewal and modernization. The reason for this is the security situation in the world at large. We can now create a modern, flexible and versatile defence on the basis of national service. The units and systems that will be needed in the future should be capable of being utilized for both the defence of Sweden and participation in international operations.

Sweden recognises that the decades-long threat from the Soviet Union is now gone. This recognition, together with Sweden's entry into the EU, means that Sweden's defence policy is still undergoing important changes. The military is committed to the introduction of network-based concepts as it evolves into a 21st-century force. Although it will be considerably smaller than the Swedish military of most of the 20th century, the new force is envisioned as being very high-tech, its operations enabled by a high degree of networking.

The Swedish government envisions that, in 2004, it will make important decisions that will guide the future structure and orientation of the Swedish armed forces. Four broad policy options, detailed in Chapter 2, are being considered. Three of the four options place considerable emphasis on coalition military operations outside Sweden. Deciding which option to focus on will provide guidance to the armed forces on the direction they will take in the next 10 to 15 years.

Additionally, this decade will see considerable research, experimentation, and demonstration of future force design options, including various degrees of networking of the armed forces.

About This Report

Chapter 2, which follows this introduction, describes network-based operations. General concepts are reviewed, as well as the current state of thinking about military networking within the U.S. military and the applicability of these concepts to Sweden's military transformation. The remainder of the report proposes a methodology for assessing networked operations. The methodology assumes that the operational functions have been prioritised and that networks have been proposed to support the operational functions. Chapter 3 discusses various categories of network interaction needed to support operational functions. These interaction categories support the identification of common subnetworks and of analogous systems or components in the cost-estimation process. In Chapter 4, several operational functions that could be included in a Swedish military system are discussed. Sweden will probably implement networking technologies and techniques gradually, so prioritising which functions will be implemented first could be an important consideration for the nation's decisionmakers. Chapter 5 addresses issues that must be considered for estimating costs. In it we review how the U.S. military costs networks and include some specific examples. Swedish defence analysts may be able to gain valuable insights from the American experience. This chapter will not actually cost a network. Rather, it will provide insights on a methodology on how to do so. The report ends with conclusions and recommendations for further study. An Appendix is included describing the relationship of the metrics presented in this report with the U.S. Department of Defense's conceptual framework for assessing network-centric warfare.

2. Network-Based Operations

Network-based, or *network-centric, warfare* is generally thought to be "an information superiority enabled concept of operations that generates increased combat power through the networking of sensors, decision makers and shooters, to achieve shared awareness, increased speed of command, higher tempo of operations, greater lethality, increased survivability, and a degree of self-synchronization" (Alberts et al., 2002, p. 2). In contrast to network-based operations or warfare, traditional warfare is considered to be *platform-centric,* in which each weapon system acts independently, so that forces must be massed to mass combat effectiveness. In network-centric warfare, effects are massed rather than forces. That is, the employment of weapon systems is *optimised* so that a target is serviced by the most effective system in the network.[1] Thus, it is hypothesised that the effects of massing force can be obtained with a much smaller force. For this reason, network-based operations are attractive to the Swedish Defence Forces.

The Network

A network is the fundamental requirement for conducting network-based operations. Consequently, it is important that we understand its components and how they interact. The language of networks is the language of graph theory applied to communications. Terms such as *directed* and *non-directed information flow, physical* and *logical connectivity, nodes,* etc., make up the elements of a network and are the basis for assessing the network's cost. We elaborate on these and other elements in the sections that follow.

A *network,* in the broadest sense, is a collection of nodes linked in various ways to one another. Individual users at these nodes can utilise these links to transmit and receive information and data, the type of which depends on the nature of the network and the requirements of the users to and from other participants in the network. This resource-sharing may require a direct connection from the sender to the receiver. However, networks often can take advantage of their overall connectivity to allow users to reach one another's assets wherever they might

---

[1] Actually, the word *optimised* is a bit strong. "Improved considerably" is closer to the truth.

reside in the overall system, whether the path is direct or passes through other users along the way. Thus, Individual A may pass along a piece of information that Individual Z may find out about, even though he/she is not directly connected to A. (Whether the version of the information that Z hears is the same one that A initiated is another matter.)

Infrastructure

By providing for the movement and storage of data, and by providing access tools, connectivity among entities executing the mission and entities peripheral to the mission, collaboration tools, and decision support tools, the network becomes the means by which the defence forces conduct network-based operations. Therefore it "enables" network-based operations. Although building such a network is costly, it is a technical problem and not an operational one. Access will vary with the mission, thus providing for a flexible network that can adjust as rapidly as required. A network manager (controller) can control access using system software.

The type of network needed to support military operations is a collection of operational, communications, sensor, and processing nodes able to communicate among each other over some communications medium. Not all nodes need to communicate with all others, and the capacity of the communications channels between nodes may vary. However, the connections among the nodes are physical. That is, a communication channel, such as a wire or an electromagnetic communication, exists between any two nodes that are connected.

Table 2.1 summarises the elements of an information network. Each of these elements contributes to the overall information infrastructure costs. How many such elements there are in a network will vary with the operational functions to be supported. The cost of multiples of these elements may or may not be additive. For example, to the extent that software is "reusable" among like facilities, development costs may not be additive. However, it is likely that maintenance costs will be.

Table 2.1

Information Network Elements

Facility	Description	Elements
Sensor	Collects information needed to support decisionmaking.	Sensor equipment Platform Processing code (software) Communications equipment
Fusion Centre	Combines reports from disparate sensors and sources to produce a common picture of the battlespace.	Terminal display equipment Decision support tools Exploitation analysts Data storage and retrieval Fusion algorithms (software) Communications equipment
Terminal Facility	Supports a subscriber by providing necessary communications and display equipment.	Terminal display equipment Decision support tools Collaboration tools Data storage and retrieval Support personnel Communications equipment
Data Storage	A database accessible to subscribers to support operations. Posting and retrieval of data are possible.	Computer data-storage equipment Data retrieval and posting tools Database management software Support personnel Communications equipment
Communications Relay Facility	A communications centre devoted solely to relaying communications between terminal facilities or other relay facilities	Communications relay equipment Support personnel Switching software Communications equipment
Network Controllers	Persons or devices that govern the operation of the network; capable of restricting use and reallocating resources.	Control centre equipment Support personnel Monitoring software Resource-allocation tools Communications equipment
Communications Transmission Facilities	Transmission media used to connect relay and terminal facilities.	Transmission media (UHF, HF, etc.) Support personnel Communications equipment

Operational Network

The operational infrastructure consists of logical connections among the entities involved directly and indirectly in the operation being supported. The communications path between two physically connected entities is of no consequence; that between two logically connected entities is. The preceding discussion of the information network infrastructure focused on physical connectivity.

The operational network takes advantage of the enablers provided by the information network to share information among collaborating teams. It facilitates decisionmaking by providing access to information to decisionmakers and by enabling the use of decision support tools. Once a decision is made, the network facilitates execution of the decision by allowing information to be disseminated, the force to be controlled, and synchronised execution to be ensured.

Figure 2.1 illustrates a notional construct of an operational network with subscribers, subnetworks, virtual collaboration teams, and network controllers, all of which entities depend on the infrastructure of the information network.

The following elaborates on the elements depicted in Figure 2.1.

Subscriber Node: One of the entities participating in an operational function. To participate in a network-based operation, the subscriber must be "network ready": equipped with a means to connect to the network in order to send and receive mission-specific information.

Subnetwork: A tightly linked set of C4ISR (Command and Control, Communications, Computing, Intelligence, Surveillance and Reconnaissance) equipment and subscribers that share common equipment and software and that are permanently dedicated to a particular function. Subnetworks are usually linked in hierarchical or distributed-network schemes. Examples are logistics networks and permanent command and control (C2) networks, such as the U.S. Global Command and Control System (GCCS). To support an operational function, subnetworks usually function within a federated network, described next.

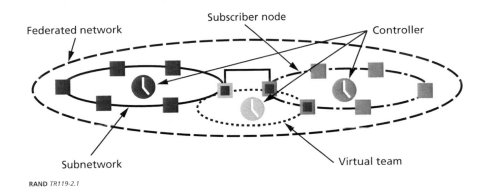

RAND *TR119-2.1*

Figure 2.1—A Notional Operational Network

Federated Network: The complete set of C4ISR equipment used by the defence forces and other users in support of an operational function. It may also include nonmilitary and non-Swedish users, depending on the mission. Conversely, Swedish subnetworks may be part of a coalition-federated network led by a coalition partner. In this way, Swedish Defence Forces are able to participate in network-based operations as part of a coalition. An example of a federated network is the U.S. Global Information Grid (GIG).

Virtual Team: A linked set of C4ISR equipment and subscribers that is rapidly brought together to perform a transient mission of a particular operational function. An example is a real-time targeting cell that combines sensors, intelligence sources, and fire-control personnel. In general, team members may be nonmilitary and non-Swedish in coalition operations. Virtual teams often consist of nodes from multiple subnetworks.

Controller, or Manager: Either a person or a device responsible for monitoring and controlling a subnetwork or a virtual team in response to environmental and operational changes. The controller is the gatekeeper as well, enforcing rules governing the conditions under which subscribers utilise the subnetwork or virtual team. The controller in an operational subnetwork performs functions similar to those of the network controller, except that the controller here focuses on operational function requirements and not the physical requirements of the information network.

In developing requirements for the information network, the operational functions to be supported by the network must be kept in mind. Conversely, when selecting the level of support that operational functions demand from the information network infrastructure, resource-constrained network capacity must be considered.

The Network Grids

In applying the general network structures described above to network-centric operations, we draw on a structural, or logical, model for network-based operations that has emerged for the U.S. Navy (Cebrowski, 1998, pp. 28–35). Its fundamental requirement is a high-performance information network that provides the capacity for computing and communications among entities participating in a given operation. This is what we refer to as the *network infrastructure*, the basic requirement for conducting network-based operations.

The conceptual model consists of three network grids: information, sensor, and engagement. In the most-common representation of the three grids, the engagement grid is shown as a subnetwork of the sensor grid, which is shown as a subnetwork of the information grid. However, the three grids can also be thought of as overlapping subnetworks of a single federated network. In Chapter 3, this view of the network grids is further extended into four interaction categories.

The Information Grid

The *information grid* provides the infrastructure to "receive, process, transport, store, and protect information for the Joint and combined services" (Stein, n.d.). It must be ubiquitous, thereby enabling the full range of military operations to experience its benefits. The structure of the information grid will determine the degree to which the Swedish Defence Forces are able to conduct network-centric operations as opposed to platform-centric operations.

The level of participation in international operations with other countries will depend considerably on the degree to which the Swedish information grid can operate with allied networks—especially those of the U.S. and European governments. For this reason, analysis should include an evaluation of the cost implications for various degrees of interoperability.

This is not a trivial consideration. The cost implications are huge. Thomas Barnett (1999), writing in the *Proceedings of the U.S. Naval Institute*, issued this warning:

> ...Our relatively rich allies fret about keeping up, wondering aloud about a day when they won't be able even to communicate with us. These states barely can afford the shrinking force structures they now possess, and if network-centric demands the tremendous pre-conflict investments in data processing that I suspect it does, then the future of coalition warfare looks bleak indeed.

Developing the information grid—at whatever level of performance—will entail a major investment even before the costs associated with the operational functions are considered.

The Sensor Grid

The sensor grid is a network that makes use of those sensors in the information grid that are pertinent to a given operational function. The sensor grid has the ability to generate high levels of battlespace awareness through sharing and fusion of information. It also contributes to effective force synchronisation. It is made up not only of typical warfare sensors, such as radar, but also of imbedded logistics sensors, such as those used to track supply. The sensor grid can be unique to each operational function; therefore, its cost can be attributed somewhat to the operational infrastructure.

To function effectively, the sensor grid must be imbedded within the information grid. The collection, processing, and dissemination of information from the battlespace require a network infrastructure commensurate with the complexity of the tasks to be performed.

The Engagement-Decision-Shooter Grid

Although the name of this grid implies combat operations, this grid is equally applicable to other military operational functions. The term "shooter" simply refers to the action component of the operation. Sensor and operational elements of the network are tasked to act in the engagement grid. This grid, like the sensor grid, is dynamic: It is able to use a unique blend of operational elements and sensors for each operational function.

As with the sensor grid, the engagement grid is imbedded in the information grid. In network-based operations, decisions can be taken at any command level. Both decentralised and centralised decisionmaking can be accommodated, depending on the operational function being supported. In either case, the decision taken depends upon the situational awareness enjoyed by the decisionmaker. Good situational awareness demands a well-connected information network.

One of the hallmarks of network-based operations is the ability to call on the best available asset involved in the operation to actually "shoot" at the "target." This is what is meant by being able to "mass effects" to achieve what, in the past, required massed force. For the network-centric-warfare concept to be effective, the necessary target information must get to the shooter, which, from the first, requires a robust information grid.

The engagement and the sensor network grids are composed of nodes represented by individual sensors, weapons, information-processing facilities, or command platforms and are connected via networked data and communication. They are not necessarily separate, but often have overlapping components. For example, the sensor grid begins a track on a cruise missile and continues to track as the pertinent unit engages and a kill is made.

Emerging U.S. Vision

Although practiced more within the U.S. Navy, where it has its origins, network-centric warfare (NCW) is emerging as a key operational concept to support the U.S. military's force transformation. In Afghanistan, Air Liaison Officers (ALOs) accompanying U.S. Special Forces troops and forces in opposition to the Taliban were able to call on orbiting aircraft to attack ground targets. They were able to do so using a sophisticated network of sensors, sources, carrier-based aircraft, tactical aircraft, and strategic bombers. The effect was the accurate and timely delivery of devastating damage to enemy positions. As a recent article in *Business Week* (2003) put it:

> The military's resounding success in Afghanistan, where units from different branches of the service worked in unprecedented unison, has led to a consensus that NCW is the way of the future.

NCW is emerging as the future of warfare in the United States military for one simple reason: From the dawn of organised conflict, military strategists have used communications and information to beat the enemy. The ancient Greeks dispatched runners over long distances to deliver military messages. European infantries used drummers to communicate common battle orders to soldiers fighting together who did not speak the same language. NCW sprang from a need, dramatised in World War II and Vietnam, to use information technology to create a more lethal fighting force, as well as to avoid casualties from friendly fire.

Getting back to the Navy, the U.S. service that has embraced NCW (or network-centric operations, NCO) the most, we cite a recent Congressional Research Service report (CRS, 2002), which stated:

> Network-centric warfare (NCW) is the Navy's central concept for organizing its efforts to transform itself for military operations in the 21st Century. NCW focuses on using information technology (IT) to link

together Navy ships, aircraft, and shore installations into highly integrated networks.

For this reason, we include the status of two key U.S. Navy NCW programmes: Cooperative Engagement Capability (CEC), perhaps the most mature NCW programme in the U.S. military today, and FORCEnet, a nascent programme designed to link sensors, networks, decision aids, weapons, and supporting systems into a single system.

Cooperative Engagement Capability

The CEC system links U.S. Navy ships and aircraft operating in a particular area into a single, integrated, air-defence network, in which radar data collected by each platform are transmitted on a real-time (i.e., instantaneous) basis to the other units in the network.

A CEC installation on a ship or aircraft includes an antenna for receiving and transmitting radar data and a computer processor for processing received radar data and fusing it with radar data collected by the ship's or aircraft's own radars.

Each unit in the CEC network fuses its own radar data with data received from other units. As a result, units in the network share a common, composite, real-time air-defence picture. CEC will permit a ship to shoot air-defence missiles at incoming anti-ship missiles that the ship itself cannot see, using radar targeting data gathered by other ships and aircraft.

The Cooperative Engagement Capability is one of the first network-centric systems that encompasses sensors and weapon systems used in the U.S. Navy battle forces. When it is successfully integrated with the air-defence systems of the other services, it will serve as the foundation for a single, integrated air picture and for weapon employment in future joint and combined operations.

FORCEnet

FORCEnet is an architecture consisting of sensors, networks, decision aids, weapons, warriors, and support systems integrated into a comprehensive system that supports all naval operations (U.S. Navy, 2002). The goal is to dominate the enemy across the spectrum of naval missions in joint, allied, and coalition operations.

The implementation of FORCEnet is the process by which the U.S. Navy plans to shift from platform-centric to network-centric operations. Realisation of this shift in warfighting capability involves an understanding of how weapons, sensors, and information systems will interact.

Sweden's Emerging Defence Policy Options

Although details are still to be worked out, Swedish armed forces' long-range planning is currently considering four major policy options (W, X, Y, and Z) for the future, which are summarised in Table 2.2. The primary difference between these options is the degree of emphasis they place on three areas: *capabilities for international operations, homeland defence,* and *adaptable structure for unforeseen future needs.* As mentioned at the end of Chapter 1, three of the four options place considerable emphasis on international operations.

In more detail, the current options are as follows:

- **Option W** devotes 70 percent of Sweden's defence effort toward international operations, 10 percent for homeland defence, and 20 percent for unforeseen contingencies. International operations in this option are focused primarily on peacekeeping and peace building, which means that Swedish military forces would arrive relatively late in a crisis, generally after combat operations have subsided. If necessary, homeland defence forces will be configured for new types of threats. This option is a dramatic change for Swedish defence policy after decades of emphasis on homeland defence.

- **Option X,** which has the same distribution of effort as in Option W, would include peace enforcement in the international effort, for which combat operations would be a distinct possibility.

- **Option Y** places less emphasis on international operations than do Options W and X, with only 20 percent of defence resources and capabilities going in that direction. Meanwhile, 20 percent is focused on homeland defence, and 60 percent, on resources for unforeseen contingencies. In this option, the international effort would also include peace enforcement and the unforeseen contingencies would focus on escalation of homeland defence requirements.

- **Option Z** devotes 45 percent toward international operations, which would include peace enforcement; 10 percent for homeland defence; and 45 percent for unforeseen contingencies. The emphasis in unforeseen contingencies is on escalation of homeland defence requirements.

Table 2.2

Summary of Swedish Defence Options

	International Operations		Homeland Defence	Unforeseen Contingencies	
Option	%	Peace Enforcement	%	%	Homeland Focus
W	70	No	10	20	No
X	70	Yes	10	20	No
Y	20	Yes	20	60	Yes
Z	45	Yes	10	45	Yes

In all cases, Sweden envisions that its future military will benefit from networking. An important consideration is the degree to which its efforts at networking should be interoperable with those of similar foreign systems. This issue will be discussed in greater depth in Chapter 4. Suffice it to say at this point that, with a greater emphasis on operations beyond Sweden, which almost certainly means operations in a coalition of some sort, it would be advantageous for Sweden to develop its military network so that interoperability with selected nations is relatively easy.

What Operational Functions?

The operational functions to be supported by network-based operations are those that support the Swedish Defence Force's full-spectrum requirements. These requirements fall into four broad classes:

Combat Operations: Functions directly related to combat operations, such as air and missile defence, and joint command and control.

Peacetime Operations: Other functions, which are more applicable to normal peacetime operations, such as supply and personnel management.

Interagency Operations: Still other functions relate to interagency operations, whereby the military has to exchange information and data with other government departments.

Noncombat Coalition Operations: Functions that include humanitarian assistance operations and assistance to local civil authorities.

Some specific examples of operational functions will be provided in Chapter 4. Within some of the major functions, such as joint command and control, are certain subtasks that could especially benefit from networking. Examples of these will also be provided.

Network Applications

Many possible military functions can be applied to network-based operations in the Swedish armed forces, as described above and elaborated on in Chapter 4. Some of the applications are strictly military, such as networking all the army, navy, and air force elements that would be required for air and missile defence—an example that has little application to non–defence agencies. On the other hand, the Swedish military could develop network functions for which data could be rapidly shared with non–defence agencies. Examples include sharing intelligence data for counterterrorism purposes or data on the location and status of military assets that can be applied to civilian disaster relief. Such a network could allow military authorities to quickly gain data on the particulars of a disaster for which military capabilities could be critical to saving lives and property.

Prioritisation and the Road to 2015 Defence Capabilities

Given the costs and technological challenges associated with creating a large-scale military network, there is a need to prioritise the effort. The defence policy decisions of 2004 will provide important guidance for the Swedish armed forces, military planners, and technologists, who can then prioritise those aspects of a military network that should receive immediate attention. Depending on where emphasis is to be placed—international operations or homeland security, peacekeeping or peace enforcement—decisions can then be made on how to prioritise those aspects of networking that should be implemented first. For example, if a decision is made to emphasise homeland security, as in option Y, network functions such as joint air and missile defence and the ability to share interagency terrorism-related data could receive high priority for implementation. On the other hand, if international operations are to be stressed, then networking functions that could facilitate multinational command and control would probably receive higher priority. Table 2.3 captures the *relative* importance of these classes of operational function and the four options discussed previously.

Table 2.3

Relative Importance of the Classes of Operational Function

Option	Combat	Peacetime	Interagency	Noncombat Coalition
W	Low	Medium	Low	High
X	Medium	Medium	Low	Medium
Y	High	Medium	High	Low
Z	High	Medium	High	Low

The resources required to develop various aspects of the network will vary according to the function. Some functions would be relatively easy to network, since the need for sophisticated and large data transfer would be minimal and security needs could be small. Other functions that require real-time exchange of massive quantities of secure data would be a more challenging and costly networking project. The prioritisation of operational functions should reflect a balance between the functions of the highest importance and those in which significant gains can be made for a relatively small investment.

Whatever decision is made, there will be a need to conduct years of development, experimentation, and testing to create and operate a sophisticated military network. Currently, Sweden plans to spend most of this decade in development and testing of options for network architectures, hardware, software, and procedures. The goal is to be able to conduct more information-rich, sophisticated military operations by the 2015 time frame.

3. Network Interactions

Network-based operations are proving to be increasingly effective in conducting military operations; consequently, there is a growing need to develop tools that allow defence analysts to characterise alternative network architectures and operating processes and assess their costs and benefits. *Assessing costs* means identifying all costs associated with each alternative network structure across the spectrum of operational functions; *assessing benefits* means developing *measures*—standards for comparison—and *metrics*—mathematical expressions that evaluate both the relative effect of alternatives and the degree to which one alternative is better or worse than another—to assess the performance of the network in support of combat and support operations. This chapter discusses possible network structures and the measures and metrics that need to be developed in relation to those structures.

Categories of Interaction

Although it may be a theoretical ideal to have all military functions available on a single federated network that is accessible by all military users, the reality is that there will be a stratification of users according to their need to have access to the data, their function, hardware and software costs, the ability of the operators to process the information, and security concerns. In most cases, the subnetwork will dictate access requirements. We refer to this stratification of users as the *categories of interaction*.

The degree of networking will vary with the operation being supported. We have identified four categories of interaction—specialised interaction, access, timeliness, and security. Clearly, additional categories could be identified if a more refined analysis were required or if the theoretical relationships between access, timeliness, and security on which the categories are based were found to be insufficient. However, the purpose of this categorisation is to facilitate cost and functionality assessment; therefore, to the extent that this coarse categorisation does not mask large cost categories, it simplifies cost estimation.[1] We assume that the operational infrastructure costs for all operations within the

---

[1] Assessment approaches are not discussed in detail. They may include analysis of both the network and the network components using simulation, such tools as throughput analysis, or comparison with existing networks or components.

same category are approximately the same.[2] However, each operational function should be examined for extraordinary infrastructure costs.

Distinguishing Category Features

The categories are distinguished in three ways: the degree of access required, including both the number of participants in the operational function and the type of data required; the security requirements; and the timeliness, or time criticality, of the information needed to support the operational function. The following sections discuss each of the four categories depicted in Figure 3.1. At the same time, Figure 3.1 is an idealised representation of the relationships among these three attributes. Category 1 is the least extreme, with low to medium requirements for access, security, and timeliness; each of the other categories reflects domains having a high, dominant, priority for either access, security, or timeliness.

In general, the number of categories under consideration is n^m, where m is the number of dimensions, or axes—three in this case: access, timeliness, and security—and n is the number of values considered for the axes—two in this case: high and not high—resulting in eight categories.

We have limited our discussion to the four categories, because we believe that they provide a useful decomposition of operational functions and to limit the complexity of the following discussions. Category 1 corresponds roughly to the information grid defined in Chapter 2; Categories 2 and 3 correspond roughly to the sensor grid; and Category 4 corresponds roughly to the engagement grid. As discussed below, we believe that these categories are all that are necessary to cover most of the operational functions.

As the need for real-time access to information increases, the number of participants in the operation requiring access to the network decreases. For example, for a cruise missile defence mission, only a limited number of participants need access to information on the network (sensors and shooters), and the information (location of incoming enemy cruise missiles) available on the

---

[2] This is an all-encompassing assumption—access, timeliness and security—and we realise that there will be differences among operational functions at roughly the same level of interaction. However, it is easier to deal with these marginal differences than to repeatedly assess *all* costs.

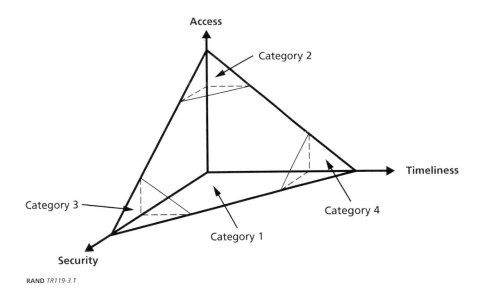

Figure 3.1—An Idealised Representation of Interaction Categories

network is time-critical. Security concerns are also limited, since the value of the information is highly time-sensitive and generally transient and perishable.

On the other hand, as the requirement for access expands to more and more participants, timeliness and security generally cease to be a prime concern, whereas access requirements increase. For example, personnel functions generally involve all commands and agencies. Although some actions may be time-sensitive or commercially sensitive, in general timeliness and security are not overriding concerns.

Similarly, as the requirement for security increases, the number of interacting participants and the timeliness requirements for information tend to decrease. Highly secure operations, such as intelligence, tend to rely on a range of information sources, including historical data, and not on highly time-critical data.

This segregation of network interactions has considerable resource implications. Although it is not necessarily true that one end of the interaction spectrum is more costly than the other, the cost categories for each interaction category are homogeneous.

Category 1—Specialised Interaction. In this category, the requirements are not as extreme as for the categories that follow. The requirements for access to information vary with participants' roles and the structure of the supporting subnetwork. The requirement for near-real-time access to information varies by participant. Some security may be required, but it is not a driving factor. These requirements for access, timeliness, and security may each range from medium to low. While this category covers a wide range of networks, many of the requirements will be trivial and not suitable for Defence needs. For example, as the level of access, timeliness, and security approaches zero, the need for any form of network disappears.

The participants on these networks generally collaborate according to a need to know and may utilise specialised manipulation tools and data stores. The networks may require a level of robustness and monitoring to meet security and timeliness requirements. We would expect that the large majority of combat operational functions would fall in this category.

For example, service and joint supply and transportation activities might require this level of network interaction. The location of transportation assets, such as ships and aircraft, plus the loads that they are expected to carry, and the timing and locations of pickup and delivery would all be included for the participants. The data would probably not have to be real-time, nor would all participants in a military federated network need to access this type of information. Rather, only those users concerned with the management of transportation assets, plus those authorised to enter transportation requests into the system, would be included. Controllers would deny access to other network users who do not have a need to participate.

Category 2—Ubiquitous Interaction. Functions that require this degree of network accessibility are those that generally affect large numbers of organisations. For example, subnetworks that support personnel-management activities, payroll, and supply functions, along with certain joint operations requiring several units from all services. In general, the several participants in the supported activity will require similar access to data and information on all aspects of the operation available on the federated network.

Time is generally not a critical factor for these operational functions. To be sure, there are deadlines; however, the need for real-time information is not a characteristic of ubiquitous-interaction operational functions. What is important is universal access, including access of a wide range of participants to a wide range of potential collaboration participants, information sources, and information-manipulation tools. Historical data are usually maintained for archival and auditing.

Category 3—Secure Interaction. Several operational functions require that both operations and information be secure, including most intelligence operations, covert activities, and Special Forces operations. Such operations place unique demands on the network for interactions among participants and the information exchanged to be secured both physically and electronically.

Adding to the difficulty is the fact that access may not be restrictive. That is, a large number of participants may require access to the network over a wide range of data sources and media, even though collaboration will normally be limited on the basis of a need-to-know. In addition, several sources of information may be required—even historical data—with some redundancy to ensure robustness. Operational functions at this level require protected sources, access, and storage of critical information. A robust network design and monitoring are needed to maintain the integrity of the network and the information on it, which inevitably lead to increases in both software and hardware costs.

Intelligence-gathering activities require analysts to access information from a plethora of sources, over such diverse media as overhead satellite imagery to written reports from covert operators in the field. All forms of intelligence—electronic, communications, optical, imagery, human sources, and the more technical sources such as ground moving-target indicators (GMTIs)—are accessed to produce a composite picture of the battlespace. The security of the information and the physical protection of the processing facilities are paramount at this level of network interaction.

Category 4—Real-Time Interaction. Operations requiring this level of support are highly restrictive, extremely time-sensitive combat actions that require that very few participants have access to critical real-time data and that those few are able to share that data among themselves, even when network connections and nodes have failed. The high costs of the required hardware and software contribute to a restriction on the number of participants. Such operations include cruise- and ballistic-missile defence. It is likely that the federated network for such operations would consist of only one or two subnetworks.

Security concerns also have a major impact here, as they did in the previous network interaction level. However, security is a transient condition: Once the information is used, its security is no longer of concern. While it would be advantageous to have certain intelligence data available on a network, concern for sources would result in a highly restricted number of entities with access to this aspect of a network.

Determining which of these four categories of network interaction each operational function requires is an early task in assessing the costs and benefits of network-based operations. To make this task easier, it is helpful to establish measures that can assess the broad interaction requirements needed to support each operational function. The degree of interaction available from the federated network is clearly a function of the structure of the available underlying information network. Therefore, the measures selected are designed *to assess the ability of the underlying network to supply the full range of information services, on demand, to the entities participating in operational functions.*

We discuss this next by focusing first on a set of general capabilities that may or may not be required to support each operational function.

Capabilities of Interaction Categories

For each capability, we propose measures that can assess the degree to which a specific operational function requires that capability. In developing these measures, we draw on the U.S. Conceptual Framework for Network Centric Warfare (Signori, 2002).[3] The framework provides a collection of application-independent metrics for the range of Network Centric Warfare capabilities. The capabilities are divided into three domains—Information, Cognitive, and Physical. A fourth, Social, domain intersects the other three.

We draw on the measures from the Information domain—in particular, those associated with Robust Networking—because our primary concern is to address network requirements and costs. However, these measures may also be useful if it is necessary to reverse-engineer specific network requirements or to understand the cost of converting operational functions to be network-centric. Measures need to be customised for specific applications. We present application-specific adaptations of the Information domain capabilities and measures that can be applied to the analysis of a network concept or design rather than a fielded network.

We have changed some of the terminology for the following reasons: The framework uses a common set of attributes across different capabilities, and we have elaborated the definitions to distinguish the metrics associated with different capabilities and to reflect the reduction in the scope of some metrics that is necessary for the assessment of network concepts and designs. The Appendix provides a detailed mapping between the framework and the metrics discussed

---

[3] This work was conducted by RAND and Evidence Based Research (EBR) Inc., under the sponsorship of the Office of Force Transformation (OFT) and the Office of the Secretary of Defense, Command Control, Communications and Intelligence (ASD/C3I), and was designed to be tailored to specific applications. More information can be found at http://www.dodccrp.org/ncw_workshop/IntroductoryBriefs/SignoriAConceptualFrameworkforNCW.ppt.

below for the Information domain: collaboration, network connectivity, discovery and collection, network control, and net-ready nodes.

Collaboration

Collaboration is a *process in which operational entities actively share information while working together towards a common goal.* More than anything else, the ability of widely dispersed operational entities to collaborate characterises network-based operations. To be effective, collaboration must allow the collaborating entities to share essential information quickly and efficiently. Collaboration processes are focused on developing a common, shared picture of the relevant battlespace.

Collaboration Capability: The capability associated with collaboration is *the ability of participants executing an operation to share information interactively over the federated network.*

Measure of Collaboration: Some operations require several units, or elements, to collaborate to support decisions, which means that several entities must have access to information and that they must have the ability to share that information among the collaborating team. The measures that assess the degree to which an operational function requires collaboration to support decisionmaking are as follows:

1. **Collaboration reach:** The number of the participants in an operational function who are required to take part, on demand, in a virtual team. In this case, a virtual team is a group of participants that is required to perform special functions outside of the bounds of their assigned tasks (see Figure 2.1). For example, a team of subscribers located at widely dispersed sites throughout the network and serviced by different communications systems is asked to collaborate to arrive at a consensus operational plan.

2. **Collaboration richness:** The amount of the network's data sources that an operational function requires to be accessed by and shared with virtual team members, subject to security constraints.

3. **Collaboration intensity:** The number of sharing modes an operational function requires its participants to have available.

4. **Collaboration timeliness:** The maximum amount of time for an interaction and response that an operational function requires.

5. **Collaboration robustness:** The number of connections an operational function requires to exist between members of the virtual team.

Network Connectivity

Two entities are connected if *there exists either a physical communications channel between the two or if the two are linked logically*. *Logical connectivity* implies that the two connected entities are able to communicate directly or to communicate indirectly through some intermediate node or nodes. As mentioned earlier, when discussing functional operations, we are generally concerned with logical connectivity. However, there may be some operational functions in which it is important to assess physical connectivity. Connectivity requirements for a functional operation are a prime indicator of network interaction levels.

Connectivity Capability: The ability of the federated network to allow participants supporting an operational function *to transmit data and information among themselves*.

Connectivity Measure: Each of the following connectivity measures has specific resources implications associated with it:

1. **Connectivity reach:** The number of network links between all participating entities required to support the operational function.

2. **Connectivity robustness:** The number of network links that can be cut without a loss of required reach.

3. **Connectivity capacity:** The number of required links supporting the operational function with capacity that exceeds an established threshold in kilobytes per second (kbps).

4. **Link security:** The number of required links supporting the operational function that allow for encryption.

These measures focus on the number and extent of the communications and information-processing assets needed by the entities participating in the operational function to collect and process relevant information and execute a decision. The number of operational entities required to provide information and to execute decisions influences the level of interaction considerably. Several units or elements may be required to operate together or to be brought together quickly in time and space to achieve desired effects (e.g., without massing forces ahead of time).

Discovery and Collection

Providing users access to information and providing a means of posting information needed by other users are important functions of a network. The ease with which a user is able to navigate the network to find the information he or she requires is a function of how the network is organised for accessing and for storing and securing data.

Discovery and Collection Capability: The ability of users *to find and access relevant information* on the federated network.

Discovery and Collection Measures: The following measures can be used to assess the extent to which an operational function requires access to information on the network.

1. **Information reach:** The number of the network's data sources that must be accessible to participants to support the functional operation.

2. **Organisation:** The arrangement of data needed to support a functional operation, measured in terms of the ease with which a subscriber can access the data with an exact query, or the number of participants for whom finding desired information with an exact query is required.

3. **Navigation:** Much like organisation, in that it refers to the ease with which a subscriber to a network can access information. However, instead of focusing on an *exact query,* navigation is concerned only with a *topical query,* which uses keywords to search for data and, hence, is less formal than an exact query. The appropriate measure, therefore, is the number of subscribers for whom finding the relevant information with a topical query is required.

4. **Storage capacity:** The maximum quantity of data that must be maintained by the network to support the operational function.

5. **Data security:** The number of the network's data sources that must be secured against outside corruption to support the operational function.

6. **Data timeliness:** The maximum amount of time between the generation of data and its transmission that can be tolerated to effectively execute the operational function.

Network Control

The management and control of a network are extremely important to network-based operations. Unfortunately, without some central control or direction, it is not possible to simply construct a network and expect subscribers to use it. This is also true for both the network infrastructure and the operational functions that use the network.

Network control and management functions include monitoring changing conditions in the network, such as diminished capacity due to overload or incapacity of some facilities; determining which subscribers should have access to other subscribers and network information, which is likely to vary with operational function; resource allocation and reallocation—for example, reassigning bandwidth to meet network demands; reconstituting the network by rerouting traffic, as necessary; and enforcing security restrictions on the network, thereby denying access to selected participants.

Network Control Capability: The extent to which a network controller *can adapt the federated network to changing mission conditions.*

Network Control Measures: The following measures for this capability are derived from the functions associated with network control:

1. **Monitoring:** The degree to which an operational function requires a network controller to detect a meaningful change in network conditions. For example, the importance of detecting outages across the network and how quickly they must be detected.

2. **Access control:** The amount of time an operational function requires for a network controller to activate or deactivate network access for a participant.

3. **Bandwidth control:** The amount of time an operational function requires for a controller to reallocate bandwidth among the network's nodes. Note that the network node is specified here and not the participant, because we expect that bandwidth would be allocated to the facility servicing the participant and not the participant himself/herself.

4. **Reconstitution:** The amount of time an operational function requires for a controller to find and activate alternative communications paths between disconnected network nodes.

5. **Access security:** The maximum number of operational-function participant facilities that cannot be penetrated by unauthorised users, due to a controller's policies and procedures.

6. **Capacity control:** The amount of time an operational function requires for a controller to add or remove a node from a network while maintaining required security and timeliness constraints. This time includes the addition of storage nodes and nodes in other networks, as required for the operational function.

Net-Ready Nodes

In addition to network infrastructure being robust, participants must also be capable of connecting to the network to support operational functions. Equipping participants to gain access to networks can add to operational costs. Net-ready nodes, another measure of network interaction, include both the participants and the equipment they need to access the network.

The level of network readiness bears directly on the level of network interaction. Some operational functions might require very little direct access to the network; others might require considerable access. We measure *readiness* in terms of the time required for a participant to access the network; the capacity, in terms of bandwidth required; the node connectivity and information accessibility required; and the level of required security.

Net-Ready Nodes Capability: The degree to which operational function participants have *the ability to connect to the network.*

Net-Ready Nodes Measures: There are several aspects of being "connected to the network," and the following measures deal with the main requirements for participants to connect to the network:

1. **Access time:** The maximum amount of time an operational function can allocate for a node or participant to connect to the network.
2. **Participant capacity:** The maximum bandwidth an operational function requires to be addressable by nodes or participants in the operation.
3. **Node connectivity:** The minimum number of media modes (modem, on-the-move wireless, high-bandwidth wire, etc.) an operational function requires its nodes or participants to access.
4. **Information accessibility:** The number of information format types (HTML, XML, VMF, etc.) that an operational function requires the nodes or participants to support. Also referred to as *posting* and *retrieval capability support.*
5. **Node security:** The number of nodes or participants that the operational function requires to support current encryption and ID validation capabilities.

Establishing Thresholds for Interaction Categories

The capabilities and measures discussed above are used to determine the level of networking each operational function might require. Thresholds are established for each of the levels, and operations that meet these thresholds are placed at that level. Rather than establishing individual thresholds for the 26 measures, we use a two-step process: First, the measures within each capability are correlated to produce eight sets of measures that cut across all the capabilities; then, the eight correlated measures (or measure sets) are used to establish the thresholds.

Correlations

Although the capabilities and measures discussed above are useful in characterizing network interactions, the obvious correlations among the measures make them difficult to apply directly. For example, "reach" appears in collaboration and network connectivity, and "security" appears in discovery and collection, network control, network connectivity, and net-ready nodes. Operational functions requiring a high collaboration reach usually also require a high network connectivity reach. Similarly, operational functions with one high security requirement tend to have many high security requirements. In contrast, a requirement for high network connectivity reach does not necessarily imply a requirement for high network connectivity security. That is, the reach and security metrics are highly correlated, whereas the network connectivity metrics are not.

Tables 3.1 and 3.2 depict the correlations. The columns group similar metrics that are highly correlated, and the column headings are the new categories to be used for assessing thresholds for interaction categories. Rows indicate the original categories. Columns that are likely to have similar values have been grouped together. Table 3.1 shows those related to the access axis of Figure 3.1; Table 3.2 shows those related to the security and timeliness axes. Those categories in the Accessibility group of Table 3.1 concern access to information and network facilities; Reach concerns access to participants or network nodes. The Maintenance group of Table 3.2 shows those categories that are required to ensure that the security and timeliness constraints can be met. The row labels represent the capability categories discussed earlier. The table entries are the measures in each capability that correlate with the revised categories.

Table 3.1

Measure Correlations—Access

Information Capability	Accessibility			Reach
	Intensity	Capacity	Richness	
Collaboration	Collaboration intensity		Collaboration richness	Collaboration reach
Discovery and Collection	Organisation Navigation	Storage capacity	Information reach	
Network Connectivity		Connectivity capacity		Connectivity reach
Network Control		Capacity control		
Net-Ready Participants	Access time Participant capacity Node connectivity Information accessibility			

Table 3.2

Measure Correlations—Security and Timeliness

Information Capability	Maintenance		Security	Timeliness
	Monitoring	Robustness		
Collaboration		Collaboration robustness		Collaboration timeliness
Discovery and Collection			Data security	Data timeliness
Network Connectivity		Connectivity robustness	Network link security	
Network Control	Monitoring	Bandwidth control Reconstitution	Access control Access security	
Network-Ready Participants			Node security	

Developing a Measure Scale

The next step is to convert the measures to metrics by defining a scale that can be applied to each measure. We select an ordinal scale: "low," "medium," and "high." For each of the measures, we now define the criterion for each to assume one of these three points on the scale. At this stage, the criteria are rather subjective and therefore a qualitative metric is justified. In application, it may be possible to quantify the metrics. Tables 3.3 and 3.4 record the criteria.

Table 3.3

Measure Scale Criteria—Access

Access Measure	High	Medium	Low
Intensity	Access to the full range of media and media formats. Facilities for converting information between formats or viewing and manipulating information in different formats.	Access to a range of media and data formats is required. Specialised manipulation tools may be required.	The mode of data and information delivery is restricted to a few key modes.
Capacity	Storage of large volumes of information, and the ability to connect to a range of data sources, storage facilities, and interactive nodes.	Specialised information is stored, and the ability to connect to related data sources, storage facilities and interactive nodes.	Information is transitory. Storage requirements are limited.
Richness	Access to a wide variety of information that may be used for a range of purposes. Information requirements may not be predetermined.	Information on specialised topics.	Restricted to critical information.
Reach	Able to connect to and collaborate with a wide range of nodes.	Able to connect to and collaborate with a range of nodes operating within a specialised area.	Able to connect to and collaborate with a few key participants.

Table 3.4

Measure Scale Criteria—Security and Timeliness

Security and Timeliness Measure	High	Medium	Low
Monitoring	Quickly identify changes to network connectivity and access, to meet operational requirements.	Identify and fix changes to network connectivity in a timely manner to meet operational requirements.	Changes to network connectivity and access have little impact on operational requirements.
Robustness	Network must be highly resilient to failures in nodes or connections. Network performance (data integrity, security, and timeliness) must be maintained under attack.	Network must be resilient to failures in nodes or connections. Some degradation in performance is acceptable.	Failures in network nodes or connections have limited impact on operations.
Security	Secure, *both* physically *and* electronically, interactions amongst participants, the data exchanged, the information stored on the network, and, possibly, the network sensors. Network controllers strictly control access to the network.	*Protect, either* electronically *or* physically, interactions amongst participants, the data exchanged, and the information stored on the network, all of which are. Network controllers can deny access.	No security implications. Access to the network is generally available.
Timeliness	Interactions amongst participants and the provision and exchange of data must meet strict real-time requirements.	Interactions amongst participants and the provision and exchange of data must meet near-real-time constraints.	No implications due to time constraints.

Establishing Thresholds for Interaction Categories

Next, we applied the metrics to the interaction categories to determine reasonable thresholds for assigning operational functions to the four categories. The threshold sets for each operational function, in Table 3.5, establish the function's network interaction category. These thresholds reflect the theoretical relationships between access, security, and timeliness shown in Figure 3.1. However, since the criteria established in Tables 3.3 and 3.4 are, as previously stated, rather subjective and purely qualitative, this table should be considered a rough approximation. Nevertheless, the threshold sets provide guidance in assessing the degree of support that will likely be required for each operational function to be executed on the federated network.

In general, all operational functions satisfying the values for the support-requirement thresholds for a given category of network interaction are classified at that category. However, operational functions are not precluded from straddling the four categories. Such functions need to be addressed individually. If such straddling occurs often, then either the criteria are not reflective of the categories or the metrics applied require adjustment.

Table 3.5

Determining Interaction Category Thresholds

Criteria	Category 1 Specialised	Category 2 Ubiquitous	Category 3 Secure	Category 4 Real-Time
Intensity	Medium	High	Medium	Low
Capacity	Medium	High	Medium	Low
Richness	Medium	High	Medium	Low
Reach	Medium	High	Low	Low
Monitoring	Medium	Low	High	High
Robustness	Medium	Low	High	High
Security	Medium	Low	High	Medium
Timeliness	Medium	Low	Medium	High

4. Networked Operations

We now consider the implications of the four Swedish policy options introduced in Chapter 2. The four options vary the commitment that Sweden gives to international peacekeeping and peace-building; international peace enforcement; homeland defence; and either international or homeland unforeseen contingencies. Each of these commitments implies a set of operational functions, which belong to one of the four interaction categories. For example, air and missile defence is a Category 4 function that is more important to homeland defence than to international peacekeeping. Thus, the analysis of Category 4 requirements is more important for homeland defence and combat operations that may take place in peace enforcement than in international peacekeeping.

Evaluating a federation of networks involves identifying the operational functions to be conducted by each network and the corresponding interaction categories. Each constituent network is evaluated against the requirements for the interaction category, as well as any specific requirements for the relevant operational functions. The results of these analyses are combined according to the relative importance of the operational functions, which is given by the contribution of each function to the commitments and the relative importance of the commitments as given in the options.

Note that analysis of operational functions may need to factor in the desired operational context or operational concepts. For example, the main characteristic of unforeseen contingencies is an increase in force size, although an increase in the access requirements may also be required. The main network property required is adaptability, as captured in the access control and capacity control measures.

In all these functions that could be included on a military network, an overarching consideration for Sweden is the degree of multinational interoperability that is desired or required. Sweden is now a member of the European Union, including its military arm. Three of the four Swedish Defence options place a heavy ($\geq$45 percent) emphasis on international operations. Sweden will probably be conducting more coalition military operations than has been the norm for the past two centuries. Therefore, considerations of coalition force requirements and compatibility should be included in military networking decisions.

To conduct a network assessment for international operations, it is necessary to know how Sweden intends to operate in a coalition. Possibilities range from providing a largely independent force that can perform a range of operational functions in support of coalition objectives without the resources of other nations, to providing force elements that depend on force elements from other nations for mission success. These two extremes have very different interoperability requirements.

Achieving a high level of interoperability for international operations may also require an adaptable network—one requiring increased access control and capacity control—since coalition partners will not be constant and since Sweden will have no control over their capabilities.

Interoperability

The NATO definition of *interoperability* is the "ability of alliance forces, and when appropriate, forces of partner and other nations to train, exercise and operate together in the execution of assigned missions and tasks" (NATO, 2003). However, interoperability is not just a concern for international operations. Interoperability between joint force elements, government departments, and non-government organisations is also important in homeland defence, and it can be difficult to achieve, as interoperability issues among the U.S. military services demonstrate (European Institute, 2002, p. 2).

Interoperability is about more than just the ability of different nations or services to connect their systems and exchange information. In addition to the technical issues, important doctrinal, organisational, and cultural issues need to be addressed. A pair of models that capture both the technical aspects and the organisational aspects is the Levels of Information Systems Interoperability model (U.S. CRISR Working Group 1998, 1998) and the Organizational Interoperability Model (Clark and Jones, 1999) (LISI-OIM group) as used by Clark and Moon (2001). Both models have a number of dimensions and a method for ranking the actual, or required, level of interoperability.

The LISI model comprises four dimensions: (1) *Infrastructure,* which covers the compatibility of network hardware and software; (2) *data,* which covers both data formats and models; (3) *applications,* which covers the ability of applications to share and exchange data; and (4) *procedures,* which covers security and common operating pictures through to enterprise-wide procedures, which might correspond to procedures for specific operational functions. The OIM comprises four levels: (1) *preparedness,* which covers doctrine, experience, and training for the operational functions; (2) *understanding,* which covers information- and knowledge-sharing, from a policy perspective rather than a technical perspective; (3) *command style*, which includes roles, responsibilities, and approaches to delegation; and (4) *ethos*, which includes trust, culture, values, and goals.

The OIM is related to the capability of the network, because the organisation and doctrine for operational functions will depend on the network and on the level of technical interoperability. For our purposes, if Sweden wishes to be interoperable with other countries conducting network-centric operations, the most important OIM consideration is that Sweden needs to invest in network technology, compatible doctrine, and training and exercises with relevant forces. If, in contrast, Sweden envisages working with countries with limited networking capabilities, then network integration is a lower priority.

In contrast, the LISI model is dependent on the network and the operational functions that it supports. A mapping between the LISI constructs and the capabilities and associated metrics used in this document is provided in Table 4.1. The greater the level of interoperability required, the higher the required values of the metrics will be. In addition, the metrics capture only the level of network performance, not the appropriateness of such performance. For example, simply having the ability to use a large number of data formats is not sufficient if a military organisation needs to operate with another organisation that has access only to a specific data format, such as the J-series messaging used by Link 16.

The difficulty with assessing the appropriateness of the network from an interoperability perspective is that Sweden has little or no control over the capabilities of other nations. There is limited standardisation among the nations with which Sweden may want to enter into a coalition, so interoperability across a range of formats, modes, and systems is required. Furthermore, since the entire European defence budget is only two-thirds the U.S. budget, U.S. systems tend to evolve at a faster rate than the European systems, placing a substantial burden on adaptability and evolution if interoperability with the United States is desired (European Institute, 2002, pp. 3, 26). Despite calls for increased standardisation (European Institute, 2002, p. 3), such standardisation is not likely to occur because it tends to be based on widespread, accepted technology to delay the introduction of new, improved technologies and equipment.

Table 4.1

Components of the LISI Model and Associated Metrics

Component	Metrics	
Infrastructure	*Network Connectivity*	*Net-Ready Nodes*
	Connectivity capacity	Access time
	Connectivity reach	Participant capacity
	Connectivity robustness	Node connectivity
	Network link security	Information accessibility
	Connectivity timeliness	Node security
Data	*Discovery and Collection*	
	Information reach	
Applications	*Collaboration*	*Discovery and Collection*
	Collaboration intensity	Organisation
	Collaboration richness	Navigation
	Collaboration reach	Storage capacity
	Collaboration robustness	Data timeliness
	Collaboration timeliness	
Procedures	*Network Control*	*Discovery and Collection*
	Access time	Data security
	Access control	
	Access security	
	Capacity control	
	Monitoring	
	Bandwidth control	
	Reconstitution	

The metrics discussed in this document, including those related to the adaptability of the network (access control and capacity control), provide a degree of assessment of interoperability. However, if a high level of interoperability is required and if specific interoperability concerns can be identified, they also should form part of the analysis.

Illustrative Operational Functions

We now examine various operational functions that could be included in a Swedish military network. Many operational functions can be successfully executed in a network-based environment, and we make no attempt to list them all here. Nevertheless, those selected provide examples of the kind of functions that could be networked and the interaction category they are likely to be placed in. The description and rationale for categorisation of each of the other operational functions are brief and still require more rigorous analysis.

In theory, all relevant military information is available for users to access. Under ideal circumstances—i.e., assuming no budget or technology constraints, adequate security procedures, and a universal need to know—all participants in the network could gain access to and use any function in the network. In reality, the number of users for a particular function will be limited by need-to-know, cost constraints, available hardware and software, and other considerations.

Depending on the guidance from the 2004 defence decision, operational functions could be prioritised for development and inclusion in a military network. For example, in those options where international operations are to be emphasised, functions that would be applicable for the command, control, and interaction of Swedish forces in a multinational coalition would be most appropriate for early inclusion in a Swedish military network. On the other hand, if homeland defence is to receive priority then functions most closely associated with that mission should gain greater priority as the Swedish Armed Forces move toward greater network capability.

Air and Missile Defence

An operation that is highly time-sensitive and requires close joint integration among the elements of all the services that are participating (e.g., ships and aircraft), air and missile defence is a very challenging networked function. An example is the U.S. Navy's Cooperative Engagement Capability, mentioned earlier, for which multiple ships, sensors, and command elements are to be networked to allow for rapid engagement of missile threats. Sweden is currently studying options for a future air and missile defence system that would be similar in many ways to the CEC. The time sensitivity of this function is Category 4, for which seconds and minutes are of the essence and in which the number of participants is restricted to the relevant sensors and ships able to engage enemy missiles, in order to successfully defeat an enemy air and missile threat.

The Joint Air-Land-Sea Battle Command System

The Joint Air-Land-Sea Battle Command System is an example of a combat-related, Category 3 function. To provide a common operational picture to commanders and staffs, data on friendly and enemy elements, among other things, would be exchanged among all the elements of a joint force. A current example is the U.S. military's ability to provide a common "air picture" to all elements of the joint force. In the United States, Air Force Airborne Warning and Control System (AWACS) data are transmitted via the Link 16 Data Link system to the Army and Navy, thus providing them the real-time status of all friendly and enemy air elements. This system also has exacting timelines, measured in minutes. This joint command system could include various subtasks that could receive special attention for development in a network. Examples of specific functions include the following:

- **A joint targeting grid** is a Category 4 function that provides appropriate command elements of a joint force (Army, Navy, and Air Force) with the ability to share target data that are gathered by sensors from any service. Target-weapon allocations are based on the assets of all the services and could be made automatically. The function would include the ability to distinguish between friendly troops, enemy troops, and noncombatants. A current example of this kind of capability is the U.S. Air Force's Joint Surveillance Targeting and Attack Radar System (JSTARS), which was developed between the Army and the Air Force. JSTARS provides real-time updates on moving entities and must be acted upon within a few minutes. Unfortunately, the original system was not compatible with Navy data systems.

- **Joint casualty management** is a Category 1, specialised function. When a casualty occurs, the entire medical system (Army, Navy, and Air Force) could be alerted to that fact and assets managed in the most efficient way to shorten the time required to evacuate the casualty and ensure that the patient is transported to the optimal treatment facility. For example, an Army casualty might be transported directly to a Navy medical facility because the network had identified all Army facilities as already operating at maximum capacity. That same patient might be evacuated to the Navy on an Air Force asset that the network had identified as the optimal means for transporting that particular casualty. Such a system would require timelines of minutes to a few hours.

Peacetime Functions

Various peacetime functions could be included in a military network. Some of them would also be applicable to actual operations. The amount of detail and access each requires would influence its level of networking. Some examples are as follows:

- **Supply management** is a Category 2, ubiquitous function that would have wide applicability to most military units. In the U.S. military, new supply management concepts are based on experience gained by civilian transportation and warehousing firms that have created systems that give these firms high levels of visibility of the exact location of various goods at all times, even when in transit. Similar techniques could be used to manage military supplies in a more efficient manner. Certainly, improved levels of supply management would be applicable during actual operations, as well as in normal peacetime operations. An issue would be the level of joint visibility that such a system would require. For example, would there be an advantage to giving most Army commanders the ability to query the network for the cargo loads of all incoming ships and aircraft moving supplies?

- **Training status of individuals and units** is information that would be available to commanders and staffs who might need to enlist/deploy individuals with specific skills, possibly on short notice. As with supply management, an interesting issue is the degree to which this data might have to cross service boundaries. For example, would the Air Force need to have access to network data on the status of the training of an Army or Navy unit or an individual?

Interagency Operations

Operations between the military and nonmilitary government agencies could also be included on a military network. Although nonmilitary organisations possess expertise in their specialty area, they can easily be overwhelmed and require military assistance. Numerous examples can be given of military participation in medical emergencies, disaster relief, and riot control. The following are just a few:

- **Tracking terrorist organisations** requires that data from several sources be compiled and analysed. Access to several sources of intelligence would be necessary to uncover terrorist attacks planned by these organisations. An example is the cooperation in the United States among the various intelligence-gathering and law-enforcement agencies following the events of September 11, 2001. To protect sources and ensure that the terrorists do not discover that they have been detected, security is also an issue in gathering intelligence. Timeliness is also essential so that action can be taken to thwart terrorist attacks before they are executed and to warn the public. All of these factors point to a Category 1 function.

- **Disaster relief operations** also require compiling data to quickly respond to the emergency. The source of the data will vary with the nature of the emergency, but it will likely include the type of information generally compiled by national emergency-response organisations, such as paramedics, fire brigades, and police. Examples of the type of information required include the location of emergency relief supplies, the capacity of medical facilities, and data on transportation networks, to name a few.

  The military may also be called upon to assist when the disaster threatens to overwhelm civilian agencies. Timeliness and broad access to multiple sources of information and responding organisations are required. However, neither of the time requirements is extremely demanding, thus placing disaster relief operations in Category 1.

- **Mass casualty response** is much like disaster relief, but it is dominated by medical assistance—largely medical personnel and ambulance services, to include military medical corps personnel. Thus, access is limited to these organisations. As with disaster relief, timeliness is important. The military medical community describes the first hour after an injury as the "golden hour," during which life or death can depend upon whether a patient receives medical attention. Yet, this time frame is not high as high a priority as the milliseconds to seconds response times required for air and missile defence. Security is clearly not a major issue. Therefore, mass casualty response operations fall into Category 1 as well.

Applying the Metrics

We now consider three operational functions in more detail, including a discussion of their requirements and possible operational concepts.[1] The first two functions, air and missile defence and Air-Land-Sea Battle Command, come from different interaction categories. The third operational function, joint targeting, discusses a subfunction with an interaction category different from its parent function, Air-Land-Sea Battle Command.

Air and Missile Defence

The *air and missile defence function* is a challenging military operation that is very time critical and technically difficult to execute. Measured in portions of seconds and minutes, timelines are exacting. As Figure 4.1 shows, there are various

---

[1] An analysis of the relationships between the requirements, operational concepts, and network architectures will be covered in a separate report.

options for networking this function. Depending on the option selected, the data and processing requirements could be enormous. In Sweden's case, the air and missile defence network function would probably require the networking of elements of the Army (land-based sensors and interceptors), Navy (ship-based sensors and weapons), and the Air Force (airborne sensors and fighter-delivered weapons).

The U.S. Navy's network-centric CEC concept might be the model for such a system. Currently, CEC is, essentially, a Navy-only system, with minimal participation by the Army and Air Force. Sweden's national air and missile defence system would be more ambitious, since it would probably have to include elements of all the services.

Such a system might be for Sweden only, designed only for national defence, not for coalition operations, in keeping with Sweden's tradition of nonalignment. Such a system could be optimised for Swedish needs and existing systems. However, if overly optimised for Sweden-only operations, the system could be sufficiently incompatible with possible coalition partners that multinational operations would be hindered.

In assessing this function in terms of which network interactions category would be appropriate, we compared key aspects of air and missile defence with the interaction category thresholds shown in Table 3.5, as follows.

Intensity: An air and missile defence function requires a limited number of entities to participate in the activity. Intensity, therefore, is assessed as "low."

Capacity: The data required to perform this function is very "perishable," becoming outdated very quickly once missiles have been fired and are en route to their targets. Indeed, second-by-second updates are required, thus reducing the need to store large volumes of data. Capacity therefore would also be rated "low."

Monitoring: Exacting, short timelines are required; therefore, any change to the network's access or connectivity would greatly affect the network's ability to perform this function. Monitoring would be given a rating of "high."

Reach: Only a few key participants need to be connected and given the ability to collaborate to perform this function. Reach, therefore, is also rated "low."

Richness: Only air and missile defence–related data are needed for this function. With the possible exception of the supply status of missile defence units and intelligence data required for the missile defence function, access to most other network functions would not be needed. Richness, then, is rated "low."

Robustness: To perform this function, the network must be highly resilient and resistant to failures, including while it is under attack. Disruptions of even a few seconds or minutes could result in enemy missiles or aircraft reaching their targets. Therefore, the requirement that the network be robust is "high."

Security: The exchange of data among the entities performing this function would need to be protected, but the fleeting nature of some of the data means that extreme security measures may not be required. For example, once a particular enemy missile is fired, it will either be intercepted or it will reach its target; once the outcome is known, the data concerning that particular missile become historical. Although not a primary concern, security is nevertheless important; therefore, it is assessed to be "medium."

Timeliness: Perhaps the most important aspect of air defence operations is timeliness of response. Actions must be taken to intercept the attacking missile or aircraft in time to prevent it from destroying friendly assets. Consequently, timeliness is assessed as "high."

The overall assessment is that air and missile defence is a Category 4 function. Figure 4.1 depicts the entities that would have to be included in a notional Swedish air and missile defence network.

This diagram shows a notional, simplified version of the elements of an air and missile defence function within a network. Enemy missiles are first detected by an overhead (high-altitude) sensor of some type, such as an aircraft or even a satellite. That sensor transmits data to multiple users—the Army, Navy, and Air Force, plus appropriate command and control entities. All components engaged in the defence share a common operational picture from the start of the battle.

As the enemy missiles approach, they are detected by ship-based and airborne sensors. The data from those sensors are, in turn, shared with other entities participating in the defence. Simultaneously, data from those sensors are used in actual engagements to intercept incoming enemy missiles. Data from an Air Force sensor could be used by a ship to conduct an actual engagement, depending on the level of networking.

As the surviving enemy missiles approach the coast of Sweden (depicted by the straight line just to the right of Stockholm), they are engaged by land-based interceptors that benefited from data provided by Air Force and Navy sensors located farther out to sea (to the right of the vertical line). Possibly, the land-

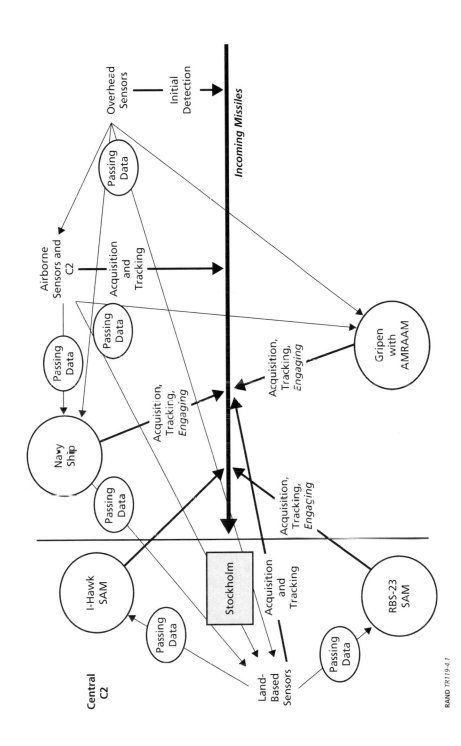

Figure 4.1—Notional Swedish Air and Missile Defence Network

RAND TR119-4.1

based interceptors fire on targets using data from Navy sensors, before their own ground-based radars acquire the incoming missiles.

Overseeing the entire process is a joint command and control entity that shares the same common operational picture that the service elements have. In the diagram, this is the "Central C2" entity.

Several options are available for the design of an air and missile defence network function. The degree of centralised control and whether the individual units (ships, aircraft, and land-based firing units) would require highly detailed target tracking–quality data of the type the U.S. Navy envisions for the CEC system would determine which option was chosen.

Option 1 is based on *decentralised* command and control, including engagement authority, *with shared target-track data.* For example, all defencive elements have access to target track–quality data on the approaching missiles, and, by using this shared, high-quality data, have the ability to engage targets without seeking prior approval. An example would be a Navy ship engaging enemy missiles by using track-quality data provided by an Air Force sensor platform. The network would provide all "users" with track-quality data.

Option 2 also has *decentralised* command and control. Therefore, as a firing element acquires an incoming missile, it can engage it without having to ask permission. However, there is *no shared track-quality data* on the network. In this option, the network would provide a common operational picture to all entities participating in the defence, but it would require each defencive entity (ship, aircraft, or ground-based battery) to actually acquire the approaching missiles with its own tracking radar and generate its own data for an intercept.

Option 3 assumes *centralised engagement control* through the network and that *track-quality data are shared.* In this case, the network alerts all defensive entities to the approach of the threat and disseminates high-quality data on the enemy missiles. However, individual defensive firing units are centrally controlled via the network; each defending ship, aircraft, and ground-based firing unit fires only when the network control tells it to.

Option 4 includes centralised control of firing elements; however, it does not provide shared track-quality data. The central defensive command and control agency manages which units will fire, via the common operational picture provided by the network. Once a firing unit has been identified, before it can fire it must generate its own target-quality data on the enemy missiles, using its own, on-board sensors.

Depending on the option selected, the network could be developed and appropriate hardware and software provided for all the required participants. The network could include the ability to change between options, depending on the specifics of the operational situation. For example, in some circumstances there would be a need for considerable centralised control; in others, a decentralised approach could be required. The air and missile defense functional options (more or less centralised control, ability to pass track-quality data) would then be assessed in terms of the measures in Tables 3.1 through 3.4.

Air-Land-Sea Battle Command

This is another example of a high-value operational function that could be included in a military network. A battle command system such as this would provide a common operational picture in near-real-time to all elements of a joint force.

The timelines required in this system would not be as exacting as those in the air and missile defence example, in which every second is precious. Nevertheless, many aspects of this system could require frequent updates and, therefore, the transmission of data on the friendly and enemy situation, as follows:

- Locations of all friendly and enemy elements

- A real-time air situation, including the precise locations of all aircraft, unmanned aerial vehicles, and missiles

- The status of friendly forces, such as unit strength, readiness for operations, and availability of all classes of supply.

In terms of coalition operations, such a Swedish system should have an appropriate level of compatibility with possible coalition partners. For example, several European nations are working on integrated, networked military command and control systems. Now that Sweden is a member of the EU military force, compatibility with similar systems of other EU members may be appropriate. The upcoming decision on which option of the four options Sweden will pursue for defense planning (W, X, Y, or Z) could provide guidance on the degree of multinational interoperability that will be required.

By 2015, a few nations' military forces will be highly networked. Technological and resource constraints will mean that most nations will not be networked. Therefore, Swedish units that could be employing a highly networked command and control system such as the one illustrated here might have to operate alongside a wide variety of coalition forces of greatly different capability.

We now assess this operational function in terms of which network interaction category would be most appropriate, according to Table 3.5.

Intensity: An Air-Land-Sea Battle Command Network would have to include appropriate headquarters and other elements to ensure the desired level of joint interaction in what could be a fast-moving situation. Although more elements would be required than for the missile defence function, this command would hardly be a ubiquitous function. Consequently, intensity is assessed to be "medium."

Capacity: Selected amounts of data would be required to perform the command function. While some of the data would have to be stored for long-term use, many data would be perishable: Once a decision is made and executed, the issue is past and the details need not be retained or archived. Therefore, this attribute is also assessed to be "medium."

Monitoring: Given the criticality of ensuring that all the required command elements know how the situation is developing and what, if any, changes have occurred in the senior commander's intent, changes to the network's access or connectivity would significantly affect its ability to perform the command function. Consequently, monitoring is assessed to be "high."

Reach: Only a few key participants need to be connected and given the ability to collaborate to perform this function. Therefore reach is "low."

Richness: The command function could require access to a wide variety of information sources. Thus, richness is assessed as "high."

Robustness: To perform the command function, the network must be highly resilient and resistant to failures. Redundant paths are essential to ensure survivability. Therefore, robustness is assessed to be "high."

Security: History includes many examples of the disastrous effects of an enemy being able to intercept data from command networks. Therefore, ensuring the security of a command function is deemed "high."

Timeliness: In combat, timely decisions are essential to ensure that command directives can be executed synchronously. In most cases, these requirements are not as strict as those for the air and missile defence function. Therefore, timeliness is assessed to be "medium."

Note that both richness and security are rated "high." Nevertheless, the other measures are rated consistent with Category 3. This is an example of an operational function that does not map uniquely into one category. In this case, we would assess the function as being in Category 3, then would deal with the discrepancies separately.

Figure 4.2 shows how the ground component of such a network function might be organised.

In the figure, a Swedish mechanised infantry battalion is operating as part of a multinational force, which includes high-tech American forces as well as low-tech partners who are not networked. The Swedish and American units can operate in a very dispersed mode, owing to the high levels of information available through their networked command and intelligence systems, whereas the other nation's forces must operate in a more traditional, linear manner.

Land-component and joint sensors locate enemy forces and broadcast their data onto the network, where Swedish forces can access it, assuming security and agreed-upon technical protocols are in place. Simultaneously, sensors organic to the Swedish battalion locate enemy forces and place those data on the network, where higher command and adjacent American units can access it.

The Swedish unit's command and control system is networked with the multinational brigade and division commands. Fire-support requests can be processed via the network to either organic land component fire support systems and/or the air and maritime components that are providing support to the land command. With the exception of the "low-tech" elements of the force that lack the appropriate systems, all elements of the multinational force share a common operational picture via the data available on the network.

As with the air and missile defence example, important decisions will have to be made regarding the construction and management of the network for this function. Paramount to the decisions would be the degree of centralisation that is desired or required. Options might include the following:

Option 1 assumes complete information-sharing among all the elements of a joint force. Total database sharing among the service components would be effected via the network, and databases could include administrative data, such as readiness, the supply situation, and personnel status. In effect, any Army battalion commander could search the military network for data on what any ship in the operational area is carrying. This level of interservice networking would require compatible software and hardware, plus shared procedures and protocols. Constantly updated operations-related information would be available through the network and would include friendly and enemy locations.

52

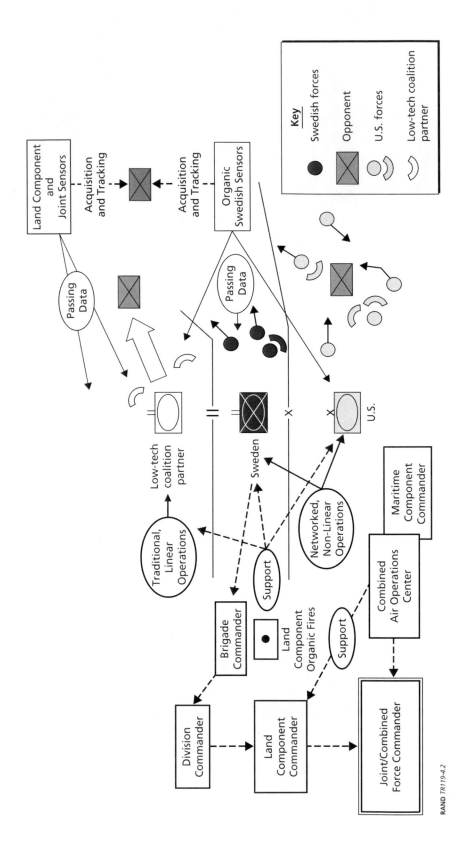

Figure 4.2—Notional Swedish Air-Land-Sea Battle Command Network

RAND *TR119-4.2*

Option 2 is not quite as ambitious. Only operations-related data would be included on a joint network. Such data could include weapon status, friendly and enemy locations, data on coalition forces, and weather information. Service-specific administrative data, such as personnel status, would not be available to the other service components.

As was mentioned earlier in this chapter, the 2004 decisions on the strategic direction of the Swedish armed forces will help prioritise networking efforts. The example above assumes that Sweden decides to emphasise international operations, including the challenging combat-like peace enforcement function. If options that include the need for multinational peace enforcement operations are preferred, then Sweden will have to consider the degree to which its own networked command system will be interoperable with those of select foreign militaries.

A Joint Targeting Grid

Joint targeting is an operational function that, within a joint command, would be used to provide the ability to assess targeting data from sensors of all the services. For example, a joint headquarters, plus Army and Navy elements, would see the same data derived from an Air Force platform. Target-weapon allocations would be based on all the available joint assets, as identified on the network. The most efficient and effective weapons would be paired against a target. It would not matter whether the weapons were launched from the air, from a ship, or by a land-based unit.

The system would require the ability to rapidly distinguish between friendly, enemy, and noncombatant elements as part of the assessment process. Such a system may have to be interoperable with similar systems of coalition forces, especially if ground and air units are employing futuristic, nonlinear tactics. This operational function can also be assessed in terms of the criteria in Table 3.5, as follows.

Intensity: A joint targeting function would require fewer entities to be involved than in a joint command function, since it is a more specialised function. Intensity therefore is assessed to be rather "low."

Capacity: Although in the other analysed functions, most targeting information has been presented as being perishable and fleeting, it is not always so. Some targets are fixed, and data on them can be stored for long periods. Therefore, this function would be assessed as being either "medium" or "low."

Monitoring: Owing to the time sensitivity of most targeting data, changes to the network's access or connectivity would have an irreversible effect on the ability of the network to perform the targeting function. Monitoring, therefore, is assessed to be "high."

Reach: Only a few entities need to collaborate to execute the targeting function and therefore reach is assessed to be "low."

Richness: The targeting function is generally limited to information about enemy forces and issues related to possible collateral damage to nearby civilian areas. Since the information requirements are restricted to these two categories only, richness is assessed to be "low."

Robustness: Reliability is essential to targeting. Redundant paths enable reliable information to get through and are essential to ensuring resilience should failure occur. Robustness, therefore, is assessed to be "high."

Security: Targeting relies, in part, on classified data on the enemy, plus time-sensitive updates to ensure that targets capable of moving can be engaged while the opportunity is available. Consequently, security is assessed as "medium."

Timeliness: As with the air and missile defence function, targeting is time-sensitive. Targets may move, making the target data perishable. In addition, information on the indigenous population may also be perishable, thus risking collateral damage. Therefore, timeliness therefore is assessed to be "high."

From these assessments, targeting is similar to air and missile defence. Therefore, it is classified as a Category 4, or real-time, operational function.

Figure 4.3 shows the elements that could be included in this type of networked function.

Figure 4.3 illustrates an example of a joint targeting grid. In a sense, it is similar to the system required for air and missile defence. Here, Army and Air Force sensors have located an enemy element. They exchange data and relay it via the network to a Navy ship that has not yet detected the target. Simultaneously, the data are relayed to the controlling joint headquarters. Thus, all elements in the force have a shared situational awareness.

According to the data that are available on the network, all the services have systems capable of engaging the target. Options for organizing and controlling this engagement function on the network include the following:

Option 1 places all targeting and available firing unit data on the network. All elements of a joint force produce targeting data that are shared and result in a

55

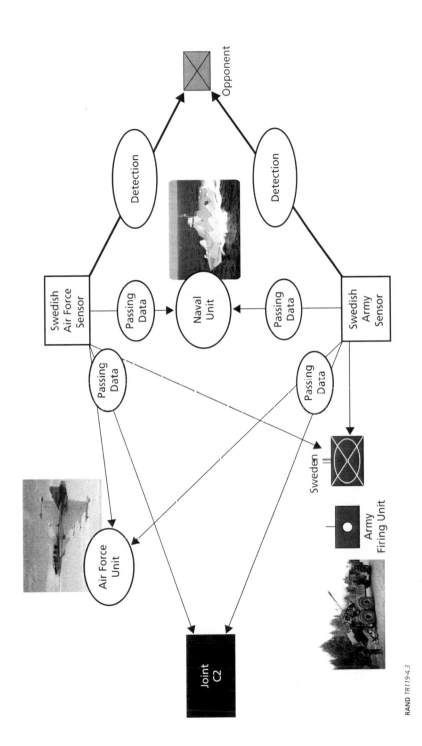

Figure 4.3—Notional Swedish Joint Targeting Grid

RAND *TR119-4.3*

common operational picture. In this option, the decision on which attack assets will engage the target is centrally managed. The central command and control hub (which would be at the joint level) has visibility of all possible attack options (Army, Navy, and Air Force) and selects those assets that will engage the target. That order is transmitted via the network. Battle damage assessment (BDA) could be accomplished by any service's reconnaissance systems, and the results of the BDA are shared with all the components via the network.

Option 2 is a decentralised version of the joint targeting grid. All elements of the joint force share sensor and targeting data, but targets are allocated on a geographic basis. For example, the Army would automatically be responsible for attacking ground targets within its boundaries. Battle damage assessment would be shared among the components via the network.

The specific details as to the degree of networking could be decided on the basis of the option selected for this function. For example, in the first option, all components and the controlling joint headquarters would require constant updates on the attack assets that each component has. The second option would not require that many data.

5. Cost Issues

A range of general approaches is available for estimating network-based operations for Swedish Defence Forces. This chapter addresses the methodology for costing network-based operations and provides background material as a preface to the methodology.

The previous chapter contained examples of operational functions that could be supported by a military network. Each network can be categorised according to the interaction categories developed in Chapter 3 and summarised in Table 3.5. The cost-estimating methodology proposed here uses the interaction categories to help estimate the magnitude of costs for each element of the network. The background begins with an introduction to general cost-estimating approaches and processes. We introduce the use of cost-element structures to ease definition and ensure consistency in estimating, and we discuss issues associated with estimating automated information systems. *Cost-element structures* represent the system in a hierarchy composed of hardware, software, facilities, data, services, and other work tasks. This hierarchical structure completely defines the system and the work to be done to develop and produce the system. We also discuss special issues associated with estimating automated information systems. This introduction is intended for readers who are unfamiliar with cost-estimating practices.

Next, we consider the lessons learned from the U.S. Navy's Cooperative Engagement Capability and the Navy Marine Corps Intranet. We present the latter network because it offers a contrast to the time-sensitive Category 4 CEC network and its relatively few participants.

The chapter concludes with a suggested methodology for estimating the cost of network-based operations in the Swedish Defence Forces.

Cost-Estimating Approaches

There are three basic approaches to cost estimating notional systems: bottom-up, analogy, and parametric. Actual incurred costs can be extrapolated to estimate the future costs of systems that already exist. The following paragraphs provide an overview of the three basic approaches and their advantages and disadvantages.[1]

Bottom-Up Approach

The bottom-up approach relies on detailed engineering analysis and calculation to estimate costs. The analyst needs complete design and configuration information for all parts of the system being estimated, to include material, equipment, and labour. The detailed design and cost estimate has as one of its advantages that many issues can be addressed, and the effect of each issue is well understood. For example, one could isolate the effect of choosing one computer processor over another.

However, the bottom-up method has the disadvantage of being time-consuming and, therefore, costly. Moreover, the system must be well-defined: There can be few unknowns. In addition, the bottom-up approach requires an extensive and detailed database of development, production, and operating and support costs for the particular technology.

Analogy Approach

With the analogy approach, an analyst selects a similar or related system and makes adjustments for differences. This approach works well for derivative systems or evolutionary improvements to existing systems. Its main advantage over the bottom-up approach is that only the changes or differences must be estimated, thus saving time and expense. However, a good starting baseline must exist to apply the method. For radical changes or new technologies, the bottom-up approach is more appropriate.

Parametric Approach

A third approach uses parametric methods to forecast outcomes. Parametric methods attempt to explain cost as a function of physical or technical characteristics related to elements of the design, such as software lines of code, data throughput, size, or weight. The relationships are frequently determined using regression analysis. These parametric relationships used for estimating costs are referred to as Cost Estimating Relationships (CERs).

---

[1] This section draws heavily on a recent RAND publication (Younossi et al., 2002).

The parametric approach has advantages for estimating costs. Principal among them is that applying the method is straightforward once the basic relationship has been defined. Unlike the previous two approaches, a detailed conceptual design is not necessary to apply the method. Another, more subtle, advantage of parametric relationships generated using regression analysis is that information can also be generated on uncertainty of the forecasted value: A result of $y \pm \varepsilon$ is obtained, where ε is related to the error terms of the regression. This uncertainty value can be just as informative as the predicted value.

While easy to apply, developing logical parametric relationships that predict accurately can be difficult, especially for software-development costs. Another disadvantage of the parametric method is the lack of direct cause-and-effect relationships. Parametric equations developed through regression analysis are based on a correlation between historical data regarding the independent parameters and the cost; they show only *associative* influences. Any forecast assumes that all the inherent relationships still apply. So extrapolating to new levels or forecasting a system with a major technical improvement is perilous. Analysts must take care not to push the parametric relationship beyond the reasonable limits of the data.

Summary of Cost-Estimating Approaches

Table 5.1 summarises the advantages and disadvantages of general cost-estimating approaches. Some of the disadvantages are particularly relevant to a methodology for estimating the costs and benefits of network-based operations for Swedish Defence Forces, which will assess numerous alternatives for operations many years in the future. Substantial detailed data, a requirement for the bottom-up approach, are not likely to be available for all aspects of the network. And the workload and time required to define in detail the numerous alternatives being considered would make the bottom-up approach undesirable.

Very few, if any, complete networks exist, with known costs, similar to the ones being contemplated—a requirement for the analogy approach.

Parametric approaches to software development require some way to size the software effort. This is difficult to do, especially for notional systems.

Clearly, each general approach has its disadvantages, suggesting that a combination of approaches may be appropriate to estimate the costs of different elements of the networked operation, based on the available data and the strengths of each approach for each element.

Table 5.1

Advantages and Disadvantages of Cost-Estimating Approaches

Approach	Advantages	Disadvantages
Bottom-up	• Cause and effect understood • Very detailed estimate	• Difficult to develop and implement • Substantial, detailed data required
Analogy	• Cause and effect understood • More easily applied than bottom-up approach	• Appropriate baseline must exist • Substantial, detailed data required
Parametric	• Easiest and cheapest to implement • Uncertainty of forecast generated	• Can be difficult to develop • Associative, but might not be causative • Extrapolation and radical changes might not be properly forecast

Further information on cost-estimating approaches and processes is available from many publicly available sources, including the Defence Acquisition University (e.g., teaching notes from Dunn, 2002).

The next section moves the focus from a general discussion of cost-estimating approaches to estimating automated information systems, of which information networks are one type.

Estimating Automated Information Systems

Each type of weapon system has its own unique challenges for cost estimation. A clear definition of the system and a comparison of similar systems or elements of similar systems are made easier by the use of a cost-element structure. This section addresses the use of cost-element structures for specific types of systems, and includes some challenges particularly applicable to automated information systems.

Cost-Element Structures

Regardless of the costing approach used, an analyst must have a clear definition of the system being estimated and must have access to known costs for the elements that make up the system. To provide a clear and consistent structure for defining tasks and estimating costs, cost estimators in the U.S. Department of Defense (DoD) use cost-element structures appropriate for the type of system being estimated, such as aircraft, missiles, ships, automated information systems, and space systems.

A generic cost-element structure for a type of system is tailored to the specific system being developed and defines all the parts that make up the system. The use of cost-element structures allows the costs of similar systems to be collected in a similar way, thereby facilitating comparison and analysis. The use of cost-element structures in the U.S. Department of Defense over several decades has resulted in a large database of contractor costs for weapon systems that is used to estimate future similar systems. A structured collection of historical costs is useful for all three estimating approaches described in the preceding section.[2]

The categories of costs shown in Table 5.2 below represent a generic cost-element structure for automated information systems. Each element can be expanded to show greater detail as appropriate. In this example, the major cost elements for Megacentre investment and system fielding have been expanded one level to show greater detail.[3]

Investment costs comprise development costs, which are one-time, or nonrecurring costs, and procurement costs, which are incurred for each system that is produced. The separation of a cost-element structure into development, procurement, and operating and support costs is influenced in the United States by laws and regulations governing the appropriation of public funds. These distinctions may not necessarily apply to other countries. What is important is not so much the separation of a cost-element structure into development, procurement, and operating and support costs as is having an overall structure to define a system that allows for comparison to similar systems, and understanding that some system elements are nonrecurring costs, other elements vary according to the number of systems procured, and still other elements represent ongoing costs incurred over the life of the system's operation.

---

[2] Information on U.S. DoD cost reporting and the use of cost-element structures is available from many sources, including the Defense Cost and Research Center, at http://dcarc.pae.osd.mil/about_dcarc.htm.

[3] Many levels of detail are possible. The authors are familiar with 7- and 9-digit cost-element structures.

Table 5.2

Investment Cost-Element Structure for Automated Information System

CES Number	Cost-Element-Structure Description
1.0	INVESTMENT COSTS
1.1	Programme management
1.2	Concept exploration
1.3	System development
1.4	System procurement
1.5	Megacentre investment
1.5.1	Capital investment
1.5.2	Megacentre software development
1.5.3	System user investment
1.6	System fielding
1.6.1	Initial training
1.6.2	System integration
1.6.3	Common support equipment
1.6.4	Site activation
1.6.5	Engineering changes
1.6.6	Initial logistics support
1.6.7	Data upload
1.6.8	Base/installation communications
1.6.9	Other
1.7	Upgrade/product improvement

Table 5.3 shows a notional cost-element structure for the operating and support costs of an automated information system, costs that are a significant part of the life-cycle cost and complement the investment costs discussed above.

As with the cost elements for investment, any of the cost elements in operating and support can be expanded in detail as appropriate to allow greater attention to and visibility of that element of cost. These are recurring costs that would be incurred in each year that the system is in operation.

The cost-element structures presented here are for the purposes of illustration. We do not necessarily recommend them for use by the Swedish Ministry of Defence. Information on cost-element structures as a management tool in commercial and government organisations is available from many sources. One example of guidance on the use of cost-element structures as a management tool

Table 5.3

**Operating and Support Cost-Element Structure for
Automated Information System**

CES Number	Cost-Element-Structure Description
2.0	SYSTEM OPERATIONS AND SUPPORT
2.1	System management
2.2	Hardware maintenance
2.3	Software maintenance
2.4	Megacentre operating and support
2.5	Data maintenance
2.6	Unit/site operations
2.7	Contract leasing

in acquiring systems for the government can be found at the U.S. Federal Aviation Administration's Acquisition System Toolset (Standard Work Breakdown Structure [WBS]/WBS Element Definitions, http://fast.faa.gov/wbs/wbssec.htm).

Difficulties in Estimating Software-Intensive Systems

A generic cost-element structure for automated information systems was shown for illustration in the preceding section because such systems are software- and information-intensive. In these respects, their costs would be most similar to costs incurred in operating the network infrastructure. Software-intensive systems have proven notoriously difficult to estimate in the United States. Many examples abound of cost growth and schedule delays because of problems in software development (The Standish Group, 1995), as do many reasons for the difficulty of estimating software costs. Among the reasons for inaccurate software estimates are frequent changes by the user, overlooked tasks, lack of coordination among organisational functions during development, and poor estimating methodologies.

Each of these causes of inaccurate estimates can be addressed. For example, a change control board that must approve changes to the system during its development can address the problem of frequent changes by the user. Overlooked tasks can be addressed by using appropriate cost-element structure to define the system and tasks. Other management tools are also available, such as a project plan, which can be used to lay out tasks, assumptions, costs, schedule, etc., for the developer and the customer. Lack of coordination among organisational functions during development can be addressed by using project management techniques, such as integrated product development teams, which have been used on successful, recent development efforts. Difficulties in estimating software systems and techniques in project planning and management are addressed more fully in *Software Engineering Theory and Practice* by Shari Lawerence Pfleeger (2001, Chapter 3).

Software-development costs can be estimated in different ways. Each way is a variation on the basic estimating approaches of analogies and parametric models introduced earlier in this chapter. Analogy approaches include expert judgment, in which a knowledgeable person develops an estimate based on his or her knowledge of the programme and the characteristics of the programme that determine software size and cost. Expert judgment may be informed by experience with analogous programmes, so that the expert compares the programme being estimated to similar historical programmes with which the expert has experience. Parametric approaches include the use of software-estimating models, which use inputs such as the number of lines of code and other parametric descriptors to generate an estimated cost.

The most crucial part of estimating software-development schedule and costs is estimating software size. This is implicitly acknowledged in most parametric models, which express software-development effort as a function of size adjusted for numerous other project, process, product, or resource characteristics (Pfleeger, 2001, p. 103). Unfortunately, it is difficult to measure software size, which means that estimating development schedule and cost is also problematic. Caspers Jones (1998), a noted researcher and writer on software quality and productivity, has written that the problem of measuring software is one of the most difficult facing the software industry.

Software is sized, or measured, by several methods. Three standard methods are source lines of code (SLOC), object points, and function points. Each of these sizing methods has its own advantages and disadvantages, and there has been a shift in what is typically used to measure software.

SLOC was the primary sizing metric when parametric models were first developed. As different programming languages and different coding processes have been developed, the metrics of object points and function points have been developed and their use has become more commonplace.

SLOC is an attempt to measure the statements, or commands, in a computer programme. Difficulties with using SLOC include that programmers use many languages to write code, and there are no rules or standards for precisely defining a SLOC in all languages; different languages can use different amounts of code to achieve the same level of functionality (Jones, 1998, pp. 104–106); and the number of lines of code required in any language is generally not known early in a development effort.

A newer method of sizing, object points are a count of the screens, reports, and third-generation language modules developed in the application. Complexity factors are used for weighting. Each object that is likely to be in the application is classified as "simple," "medium," or "difficult," and a numerical score, or weighting factor, is assigned according to the classification of difficulty. The weighted object points are summed to arrive at a numerical score. *Object points* address the difficulties with SLOC by not requiring code counts and by being able to be applied to different languages and processes. Object points can be estimated at a stage in the development effort when little detailed information about the project is available.

A third approach to software sizing is function points. Like object points, function points address the difficulties of SLOC. Function points are an attempt to measure the functionality of a system, rather than the size of the final product, which is what is measured by SLOC. *Function points* measure the inputs, outputs, interactive inquiries between user and computer, external interfaces, and internal logical files. The function points are assigned weighted complexity factors, or numerical weights, according to whether each input is assessed as "simple," "average," or "difficult." The resulting function point count is then adjusted with a multiplier for the complexity of the total proposed system. The use of function points as a metric has its disadvantages, including subjectivity in assigning complexity factors and labour-intensiveness in doing the estimate (Jones, 1998, pp. 107–109).

The difficulties in sizing software can be mitigated. When using SLOC to size development efforts, analogies or parametric relationships specific to the language and company of the system being estimated should be used. With any method, employing estimators who are certified in using a particular tool or method is advisable, as is working closely with the company that will actually be developing the software, to ensure understanding of the project.

Regardless of sizing method used, each of the approaches to estimating software development has weaknesses. Expert judgment can suffer from subjectivity of the expert and reliance on outdated or irrelevant data, or it may fail to consider factors that can affect development, such as the productivity levels of programmers. Parametric approaches are notoriously difficult to calibrate: They work best when they are based on historical programmes that are very similar to the one being estimated, and they often require an estimate of software size, which is itself difficult to determine.

Now that we have looked at the challenges in developing a methodology to estimate network-based operations, we need to look at an actual costing experience. The following section describes the cost experience with the U.S. Navy's Cooperative Engagement Capability, an air-defence network described earlier and the experience to date with the U.S. Navy and Marine Corps Intranet programme. CEC is almost certainly the most informative single programme for the purposes of assessing the costs of a network-based defence operation because its development is largely complete, it is in the process of being fielded, and it represents a challenging application of network operations. The Navy Marine Corps Intranet programme offers insights into a much different type of network that is probably best defined by interaction Category 2.

Lessons Learned from CEC and Navy Marine Corps Intranet Programmes

The Cooperative Engagement Capability is almost certainly the most ambitious and successful example of weapon system networking in the U.S. military to date, and as such offers some insights into the cost of network-based operations.[4] CEC significantly improves the anti-air warfare (AAW) capability of a naval task force by coordinating all of the force's AAW sensors into a single, shared real-time, track picture of fire control quality.[5] CEC distributes sensor data from each ship, aircraft, or cooperating unit to all other cooperating units in the battle force through a high-data-rate sensor and engagement data distribution network. The capability allows a participant in the network to engage a target even if its own sensors have not acquired the target.

The programme began formal Engineering and Manufacturing Development in 1995 (it was preceded by several years of development) and is currently in production. Development effort on the airborne and shipboard equipment is continuing. Over 20 percent of total development cost was for integration of CEC into air and ship platforms—primarily the Navy's E-2C early-warning aircraft and AEGIS radar-equipped surface combatants.[6] A constant concern was the weight and balance of the CEC equipment on the E-2C. Changes to equipment on the platforms, such as a new display on the AEGIS ships, resulted in increased integration costs for CEC.

Roughly 10 percent of the total development costs was for system testing.

---

[4] For a concise description of the CEC, see "The Cooperative Engagement Capability" (1995). For a more recent discussion, see Grant (2002).

[5] By *fire control quality*, we mean that the sensor data are fused into information that is accurate enough to be used to launch weapons at a target.

[6] Information on the share of development costs spent on integration and testing, and the proportion of development costs to procurement costs, is taken from budget exhibits submitted in the Fiscal Year 2003 President's Budget (Department of the Navy, 2003).

Extensive use of commercial off-the-shelf hardware resulted in little development cost for CEC hardware.

The largest single cost driver in development was software. Achieving interoperability and integration among various ship and air platforms was a challenge. The total software-development effort was divided into three major computer software configuration items, each developed by a different organisation or team of organisations: the Cooperative Engagement Processor, the Data Distribution System, and the Interface, items estimated to account for 24, 13, and 63 percent of the total software effort, respectively.[7]

The primary approach for estimating software costs for CEC was parametric. Estimators worked closely with the software contractors to estimate equivalent software lines of code, which was the most important input to their parametric software estimating models. The software-development costs grew over the course of the programme, primarily as a result of changes: in user requirements, in networked equipment on the air and ship platforms, and in the proportion of software code that could be reused rather than being newly developed.

The biggest costs in production are for hardware and installation of the hardware. System installation, or fielding, is considered part of production costs. Size and weight constraints on host platforms (especially aircraft) can drive production costs. The cost of each unit of hardware is less than 1/100th of the cost to develop the capability.

Operating and support costs include hardware and software maintenance, facility and site operations and support, data maintenance, and personnel costs Software maintenance and support are estimated to account for half of operating and support costs.

Continual improvements in the processing speed, and miniaturisation of microelectronics may result in platform integration and installation costs becoming smaller in the future.

The total costs and proportions of costs on the CEC programme must be understood in the context of which task the CEC network performs and how it performs the task. Of the four main military tasks performed by the Swedish military, CEC is an example within the task of defending against armed attacks. Within that task, it is assessed to be in Category 4 network interaction (real-time)—a very challenging network operational function. Furthermore, it

---

[7] Information on challenges in software development, estimating approaches to software development costs, and estimated operating and support costs was provided by a former cost estimator in the CEC Program Office, in a personal communication in December 2002.

performs the task in a highly automated way. CEC operation with the individual shipboard or airborne combat system is transparent; the network does not require any new personnel to operate it; and, in fact, the network's automation has been shown to reduce the workload on existing operators ("The Cooperative Engagement Capability," 1995). A network that performed a task that was not as time-critical or was not as automated, would very likely have different amounts and proportions of cost. Such a different network would probably have less cost for software development and more cost for training and ongoing personnel support, for example.

The lessons from CEC can be summarised as follows: Space and weight constraints on host platforms affect the development, procurement, and installation cost of the network infrastructure; changes in user requirements and other systems that are connected to the network result in increases in development costs; the variety of networked entities increased development costs; the proportions of costs among elements of the network infrastructure will differ according to the network's characteristics, such as whether it is centralised or decentralised.

The Navy Marine Corps Intranet programme, hereinafter referred to as Intranet, represents a network at the opposite end of the spectrum of interaction categories from CEC. The Navy awarded a contract to Electronic Data Systems (EDS) in October 2000 to replace an estimated 200 Navy and Marine Corps networks with a single intranet network owned and operated by EDS. As described by the U.S. General Accounting Office (Li and Brock, 2000),

> The scope of the Intranet includes everything necessary for the transmission, receipt, processing, and display of voice, video, and data—the capital infrastructure and infrastructure improvements necessary to meet quality of service requirements, as well as maintenance, training, and operation of that infrastructure. The Navy's acquisition strategy assumes that these capabilities can be purchased from commercial vendors as a service. Under the Navy's acquisition approach, the Intranet contractor will own and maintain all required desktop and network hardware and software and provide all required information technology services. The contract service area is to include the continental United States, Alaska, Hawaii, Guantanamo Bay (Cuba), Puerto Rico, and Iceland for approximately 360,000 users.

Now estimated to cover over 400,000 desktops, the contract is being implemented in phases. Implementation for a limited number of users will occur first, followed by testing and additional implementation. The contract is expected to have a value of $6.9 billion by the time it is fully implemented in 2005.

In contrast to CEC, the Intranet is characterised by high levels of intensity, capacity, richness, and reach. There are expected to be hundreds of thousands of users at hundreds of thousands of workstations at many dispersed locations. The network will connect many functions, including administrative, personnel, and supply, and will require access to legacy databases. The Intranet is much lower than CEC in its requirements for monitoring, robustness, security, and timeliness, as the consequences for delay or disruption of network services for office personnel is clearly much lower than for a military unit engaged in air defence.

The programme has encountered difficulties in implementation and has fallen behind its original schedule. The natures of the difficulties are quite different from those encountered by CEC and are understandable in the context of the network characteristics presented in Chapter 3. The primary problem is the number of legacy systems that are not compatible with the Intranet and, hence, the necessity of bringing the legacy systems into compliance: The Navy underestimated the number of legacy systems that are not compliant. In addition, local users who were happy with their service before the Intranet programme was implemented tend to be less happy with the expense and changes required to become compliant. There is cultural resistance to change from local control of the network to centralised control. Unlike CEC, the primary challenge is not a difficult coding or physical integration problem but, rather, the overwhelming number of different legacy systems operated by different local users (Verton, 2002).

A contrast in cost to CEC is that the ongoing expense of the Intranet programme for network maintenance and support is directly related to the number of users. The Intranet contractor receives payments according to the number of users supported and their satisfaction with the service. Although the operating costs of the CEC are not well known at this early stage of the programme, the programme office has estimated that software maintenance will account for much of the ongoing costs.

The costs and challenges of the CEC and Intranet programmes can be summarised according to their network interaction categories. The Category 2 Intranet programme has experienced delays in implementation and high recurring costs because it has hundreds of thousands of users (high reach) and high numbers of legacy systems and applications and need to access stored data (high intensity, capacity, and richness). The Category 4 CEC programme is networking hundreds of platforms rather than hundreds of thousands, but its high requirements for timeliness, monitoring, and robustness have driven high costs for development and for procuring each individual unit in the network.

Defence Costs Available in the United States

The preceding paragraphs have described two large and costly military networks in the U.S. Department of the Navy. It is important for decisionmakers to be able to estimate the cost of such networks so that they can assess their costs and benefits and budget sufficient funds. The ability to estimate costs accurately depends greatly on the level of detail, comprehensiveness, accuracy of the cost, and the technical data available on similar systems.

This section provides an overview of the information available to cost estimators in the United States. The intent is to provide the reader with an understanding of the types of data that are available to inform the estimating and assessment methodologies discussed later in this chapter. This summary of cost data that are available to U.S. defence analysts is presented because the quality of a cost estimate depends greatly on the cost experience on which it is based. To the extent that similar data are not available to Swedish costs analysts, the analysts may need to establish mechanisms to routinely obtain data from industry or from allied militaries.

For several decades, the U.S. Department of Defense (DoD) has required that its contractors provide structured cost reports for the weapon systems the government purchases. These cost reports are available to DoD estimators and provide an authoritative record of the development and procurement costs of major weapon systems, which greatly facilitates the task of estimating equipment costs for military operations.

Similarly, each of the military services in the United States has databases of operating and support costs for major weapon systems. These databases include the cost of personnel to operate and maintain equipment and that of their training; the cost of fuel, repair parts, and other consumable items; the cost of periodic overhaul or other major maintenance; and the cost of modifications. The operating and support costs are provided in sufficient detail to allow an accurate determination of variable costs—that is, operating and support costs that change with changes in the operating tempo of the system or the number of systems.

The recordkeeping for the cost of facilities is not as readily available, but costs of facilities can usually be found in budget documents or through the agency that provided the funds to build the facility.

Equipment and manning levels are defined by organisation and command or by geographical location. For example, an analyst can determine the maintenance manning levels for a fighter or cargo aircraft squadron, or the equipment authorised for an armoured brigade.

In addition, all costs are organised in the DoD accounting system by broad mission areas, such as strategic forces or mobility forces.

These cost records provide the actual costs of current equipment as it is currently used. Adjustments to these costs may be necessary to reflect differences in equipment or personnel on future systems. As discussed in the preceding chapter, new weapon systems can be estimated using a variety of approaches, all of which are facilitated by good, relevant cost data.

An important fact with respect to operating and support costs in the United States is that they represent almost exclusively the cost of peacetime operations, which is driven by training costs. During wartime, higher operating tempo means that costs would be higher. This distinction between peacetime and wartime operations is recognised in the ground rules of the estimate, which establish whether peacetime or wartime costs are assumed.

Historical costs are available for platforms, weapons, other military equipment, and the operation of U.S. military organisations. In practice, no individuals have access to all cost information, and any particular information is typically available to few individuals because of concerns over protecting company proprietary information or information that is sensitive for other reasons. In fact, the limited availability of cost information has important implications for estimating the cost of a new system.

In the United States, detailed technical information about the system being developed is generally available only to the organisation (usually a private company) that is developing the system and the government programme office responsible for managing the system. To protect their proprietary nature, cost and technical data are not shared widely. The amount of cost and technical data available, along with the time and resources available to perform the estimate, often determine which estimating methodologies can be used. For example, a bottom-up approach requires detailed information and the time and resources to do a detailed estimate. Such an estimate is impractical for estimators who do not have access to the detailed information or who are performing estimates of several systems as part of an analysis of alternatives or similar studies.

Swedish defence analysts who are supporting decisions on networked defence capabilities are likely to have the opportunity to perform detailed estimates only after a contractual relationship has been established with industry for such work. In the earlier stages of analysis and planning, analysts will probably rely on using analogies or parametric approaches to estimate costs. In either case, the methodology proposed in this report can be helpful.

Limitations on Lessons Learned from U.S. Programmes

The preceding sections addressed some cost lessons learned from the U.S. Navy's CEC programme and summarised the types of costs available to U.S. defence cost analysts. The lessons learned from the CEC example must be understood in the context of its unique military task and the way in which it performs that task. In addition, the lessons learned must be understood in the context of the U.S. Department of Defense, with U.S. contractors. Cost experiences in the Swedish Ministry of Defence with Swedish contractors are likely to be different.

Similar caveats apply to extrapolating from U.S. experience in all areas of cost estimating. For example, at the level of estimating software development costs for an application, many cost-estimating relationships, such as source lines of code per hour, exist based on the experience of U.S. companies. Analysts must keep in mind that these relationships are strongly influenced by a number of social factors, such as labour productivity, company practices, and the state of technology at the time, which change over time and from country to country. Similarly, at the larger level of estimating the cost of military operations, the United States has peculiarities in the way that it accounts for costs that are embodied in this methodology but that may need to be tailored for use in another country.

A Proposed Methodology for Estimating the Costs of Network-Based Operations

Assessing the costs and benefits of converting to a network-based defence structure requires a sound methodology that can help analysts to objectively compare alternative structures in terms of costs and benefits.

The methodology should have several attributes:

- It should identify all relevant costs, network infrastructure, and costs associated with operational functions supported by the network.

- It should allow for the comparison of historical and notional systems. Historical comparison provides the basis for the cost estimate, and the notional comparison allows for affordability analysis.

- It should relate network capabilities and metrics to cost in order to facilitate cost and benefit analyses.

The proposed methodology uses several steps to identify all relevant costs, allow comparison of costs, and relate network capabilities and metrics to costs. The following subsections outline the steps and provide examples of how the cost-estimating methodology would be applied. The subsection immediately following outlines the steps and provides examples for network-infrastructure costs. The subsection after that outlines the steps for estimating the costs of operational functions supported by the network. The final subsection summarises thoughts on the cost methodology.

Estimating Network-Infrastructure Costs

The recommended steps in assessing costs of operational functions are listed below. Their application will depend on the specific operational function being examined and, therefore, assumes that a function has been selected for costing.

Step 1: Define an appropriate cost-element structure for the network. This step will be an extension of the basic framework presented in Table 5.3. Network infrastructure (information-network) costs include the investment costs of exploring and defining the network concept; developing the system, including system design and specification, software development, and test and evaluation; and procuring and deploying facilities, hardware, and software. Network-infrastructure costs will also include ongoing costs to operate and maintain the network and are generally driven by personnel and software maintenance. Several of the network elements for which costs need to be estimated were summarised in Table 2.1 (Information Network Elements). This list may need to be extended as new technologies and innovations arise.

Step 2: Determine the interaction category appropriate for the selected operational functions. This means applying the measures and metrics described in Chapter 3.

Step 3: Link the capabilities and metrics of the network to elements of the infrastructure cost. We provide an example for two elements of a system, the sensors and the fusion centre for a Category 2 network and for a Category 4 network. Table 5.4 shows the costs of developing these elements of the network, and Table 5.5 shows the costs of procuring the network elements once they have been developed.

The use of the metrics for assessing categories of interaction can assist in determining at least ordinal levels of cost differences for each cost element. The example shown in Tables 5.4 and 5.5 illustrates that there are a few key cost drivers for the development of a network and that certain elements of a Category

Table 5.4

CES 1.3 System Development Costs

Network Element	Cost Item	Metric	Category 2 Network	Category 4 Network
Sensor	Sensor equipment	Timeliness	Low	High
	Sensor platform	Accessibility (Number of sensors to fit into platform)	High	Low
	Processing code (software)	Accessibility (Volume of software to support data format exchanges)	High	Low
		Timeliness (Difficult software)	Low	High
	Communications equipment	Timeliness	Low	High
Fusion Centre	Decision support	Accessibility (Number of decisions to be supported)	Low-High, depending on desired level of automation	Low, but must be automated
		Correctness (Of decisions)	Low-High	
		Timeliness (Speed with which decisions must be made)	Low	High
	Exploitation analysts	N/A		
	Fusion algorithms (software)	Timeliness	Low	High
	Communications equipment	Timeliness (Need to develop specialised equipment)	Low	High

NOTE: The two facilities used for illustration are from Table 2.1.

Table 5.5

CES 1.4 System Procurement Costs

Network Element	Cost Item	Metric	Category 2 Network	Category 4 Network
Sensor	Sensor equipment	Accessibility (Number of sensors)	High	Low
	Sensor platform	Accessibility (Number of platforms)	High	Low
	Processing code (software)	N/A		
	Communications equipment	Accessibility (Number of connections required)	High	Low
Fusion Centre	Decision support			
	Exploitation analysts	Accessibility (Number of analysts required)	Low-High, depending on desired level of automation	Low (Automation necessary)
	Fusion algorithms (software)	N/A		
	Communications equipment	Accessibility (Number of connections required)	High	Low

N/A = not applicable.

4 network can be expected to cost more for this element than those for a Category 2 network, and vice versa. Linking the capabilities and metrics of the network to the cost element also guides the choice of an appropriate estimating methodology, which is the next step.

Step 4: Choose an appropriate cost-estimating methodology. Ideally, we would like to link each cost element with its capabilities and metrics and select a cost-estimating methodology that is sensitive to the key metrics. In the example of the software development shown in Table 5.4, we would want to use analogies to similar Category 2 and 4 systems for that element, or perhaps a parametric cost-estimating relationship that used timeliness and accessibility as inputs.

In practice, the selection of the level of detail of the cost-element structure, the link to network capabilities and metrics, and the choice of estimating methodologies will tend to be determined interactively. The availability of cost data and estimating relationships tends to influence the level at which systems can be estimated. In general, logical relationships between attributes of the network and cost can and should be identified for each element of cost and the appropriate estimating methodology selected. Breaking the cost-element structure into small, component elements may allow the estimator to select analogous programmes for estimating purposes, even if the analogy was not part of a network system.

This same process is applied to each element in the network cost-element structure until the total life-cycle cost of the network is estimated.

The integration of the interaction categories with a cost-element structure in the recommended costing methodology will have one of three potential benefits to cost estimators, depending on the estimating approach used.

- When the analogy approach is used, a potential benefit is that the interaction categories and metrics can serve as a guide to selecting appropriate analogies, whether for the network as a whole or for any part of the network. For example, the analyst may be considering a network with high levels of real-time processing, monitoring, and timeliness, and need to estimate the cost to procure and install the hardware on small military aircraft. The metrics suggest a Category 4 network, for which CEC would be an appropriate analogy.

- When a parametric approach is used, a potential advantage is greater discipline in adjusting parametric models according to the metrics. Most parametric software models, for example, estimate development costs as a function of software size, with adjustments made for characteristics of the product and platform. Adjustments for increased capacity, robustness, timeliness, or product complexity result in increased costs. The metrics defined in Chapter 3 correspond closely to the adjustment factors used in parametric software estimating models such as COCOMO II (Boehm et al., 1995). The adjustment factors in parametric models can significantly affect the estimate; so, greater discipline in making the adjustments using metrics is a benefit to estimators.

- A third potential advantage in using the interaction categories is to generate CERs—the most desirable circumstance for an estimator. Enough relevant cost and technical data are available and the proposed network is defined well enough to permit the formulation of CERs between the technical characteristics of the network and the cost of the network. In this instance, the metrics provide a standard set of characteristics by which to define networks and expected ordinal relationships with cost.

Some elements may have peculiarities that affect their cost. Such peculiarities must be considered in addition to the capabilities and metrics of the network. Consider some of the major investment cost elements shown earlier in Table 5.4.

Element 1.1—Programme Management: Programme management is driven by project size and duration, as well as by the management practices of the contractor and government. Programme management will therefore be related to the overall complexity of the network. The appropriate estimating methodology would probably include an examination of staffing levels on similar defence acquisition programmes and a calculation of estimated costs based on projected staffing levels, project duration, and salary levels.

Element 1.4—System Procurement: System procurement is a recurring cost that is a function of the number of systems that are bought and the cost of each system. Clearly, the greater the number of entities that collaborate in the network, the greater will be the total procurement cost of the system. It is possible that a Category 1 network that is relatively inexpensive on a per-unit basis but is purchased for a large number of users will have a total programme cost greater than a Category 4 network for a smaller number of users.

Element 1.5—Megacentre investment: Megacentre investment may not apply if the network is operated in a decentralised fashion, as is the U.S. Navy's CEC network. In this case, the element would not be included in the cost-element structure. However, for a network that is operated in a centralised fashion and that changes significantly the way a military operation is conducted, megacentre investment may be a large element of total cost. Requirements for timeliness would likely affect the labour-intensiveness and degree of centralisation of the network by including the labour-intensive costs to develop new operational procedures and command structures and the ongoing cost to staff the command structure. If management were assisted by software, costs would be included here. Megacentre investment would include the cost to build and equip a physical structure from which the network would be managed. Using a combination of estimating methods would be appropriate, based on the labour, building, equipment, and software costs involved.

Element 1.6—System fielding: System fielding costs are driven by network size—the number of installations and platforms participating in the network. System fielding costs include training costs. If the network requires substantial changes in the way military operators perform their function, then training costs may be significant. However, a network that may be critical to a military operation may function in a way that is transparent to the user. Consequently, little additional training, or even less training than for current operations, will be required for users.

To summarise the estimation of network infrastructure costs: an appropriate estimating methodology is based on an expandable cost-element structure that includes all elements of cost, is linked to the capabilities and metrics of the network, uses the appropriate methodology for each element, and allows comparison of the costs of different networks.

Methodology for Estimating Network Operations Costs

The preceding subsection addressed the costs of the network infrastructure. These are only half of the relevant costs that should be considered. The other relevant costs are those of the military operation that is supported by the network. They include the troops and equipment necessary to conduct a military operation. It is important that both types of costs—the network infrastructure and the cost of the network operations—be considered, for two reasons. First, total costs are necessary to assess the affordability of performing the military operation either with or without a network. Sweden may also be assessing the affordability of conducting additional military operations within its new defence posture. Second, total costs are necessary to correctly assess the costs and benefits of network operations. This subsection addresses a methodology for estimating the cost of network operations.

The steps in estimating network operations costs presuppose that the military operation has been identified and the appropriate network chosen. Each military operation will have a network—at least for analysis purposes—that has the attributes of one of the four categories of networks. The unique network may share some infrastructure with other networks. For example, a network that performs a supply function may share the same fibre-optic cable lines as a different network that performs a personnel-management function. Nevertheless, the two networks are different because they transmit different data and are used by different users for different purposes. At this point in the analysis, the category of the network is no longer important because the characteristics of the network have already been identified and the costs of the network infrastructure have already been estimated.

Step 1: This step is similar to costing the network infrastructure, except that there are no cost-element structures to define which resources are needed for military operations. Just as people who are knowledgeable about networks must define the network infrastructure at an appropriate level of detail, people who are knowledgeable about military operations must define the personnel, equipment, and other resources for a military operation. For operations that are the same or similar to operations that have been performed in the past, experience serves as a guide. For operations that have not been performed in the past by Swedish defence forces, this step is more difficult and will require study and analysis to determine the resources required for new operations. Consultation with allies who have performed similar operations may be useful.

A conceptual difficulty in this step is determining what share of a person or equipment is devoted to an operation when that person or equipment performs more than one operation. National or Ministry of Defence guidance that stipulates priorities or shares of effort for different tasks or operations may aid such determinations. For example, a fighter squadron that performs multiple tasks or operations may be thought of as devoting 60 percent of its resources to homeland defence and 40 percent to coalition peacekeeping operations, and its costs would be apportioned accordingly. Further breakdowns within those tasks may be required, but the point is that some approximation of the resources required for an operation in question, including multi-mission resources, must be made.

The costs identified should include the life cycle of the system or people. For equipment, the life cycle includes development, procurement, operating and support, and disposal (which is generally negligible). For people, the costs include training, pay, travel, benefits, and retirement. The higher levels of the NCW Conceptual Framework may provide a useful list of capabilities useful in defining the cost-element structure, such as sense-making and decsionmaking, and metrics, such as *team-hardness*—the team members experience in working together—which may be required by the operation concept and for which cost estimates are required (Signori et al., 2002). As with estimating network-infrastructure costs, there is no set rule on the appropriate level of detail at which to estimate the cost of operations. A general guideline is to estimate at a level that allows identification of meaningful differences between alternatives. For example, the installation of the USG-3 equipment on the E-2C aircraft to incorporate the aircraft into the CEC network adds weight and probably increases slightly the fuel consumption of the aircraft. This difference in the cost of fuel consumption is probably too small to be meaningful in a comparison of alternatives.

Step 2: Related to the first step, this step is to determine how the military operation will be performed, both with and without the proposed network. It is conceivable that networked operations may cause a change in the resources required to perform a military operation, aside from the cost of the network itself. For example, additional personnel may be required to interpret or use the additional information provided by a network for a given operation. Or, fewer personnel may be required to synthesise or process data in a networked operation, if the network did the processing. Networking also may allow some participants in the network to have fewer sensors of their own because they benefit from the information provided by the entire network. In this way, networking would reduce the need for some equipment and associated personnel. These changes in required resources can be assessed in terms of personnel, equipment, and consumable items, such as fuel or repair items.

Step 3: In this step, an appropriate estimating methodology is selected using the logical relationships between the attributes and metrics of operational resources and cost. For example, costs per flying hour are a significant part of an aircraft's annual operating and support cost, so the cost of additional flying hours on station for an aircraft performing an operational function can be estimated using this logical relationship between flying hours and cost. In most cases, this step will be easier than estimating the cost of a network infrastructure. Personnel costs are readily estimated from well-known pay, benefit, training, and turnover rates. Equipment used in military operations generally has a long service life and so may be the same equipment as is used today. When the cost of new major equipment must be estimated, it generally has established attributes related to cost. For example, the procurement cost of a new aircraft can be estimated fairly well according to such characteristics as its weight, speed, and material composition. The scope of the costs of military operations is extensive. Capturing them all is difficult and depends upon a robust cost-accounting and data-collection system. The result of these steps will be a cost analysis of a given military operation performed with and without a network.

Additional Considerations: Finally, additional considerations must be kept in mind throughout the analysis. The analysis will be done using costs spanning a number of years in the past and future. To address the effects of currency inflation, costs should be normalised to a constant-year currency basis.

Costs and benefits will be incurred over a number of years at different points in time. To address the time value of money, costs and benefits (if quantified in currency terms) can be measured using net present value, in which future costs and benefits are discounted at a certain rate.

Another consideration with respect to time is that comparisons of alternatives may involve elements of cost that begin or end at different times for each alternative. To ensure that costs of all such elements are captured equally amongst competing alternatives, it is best to use a fixed-year basis over a sufficiently long time horizon for the cost analysis.

Summing Up

The methodology for estimating the cost of networked military operations has similar steps to those used in estimating the cost of the network infrastructure: The operation must be defined, the equipment and personnel required to perform the operation identified, logical relationships established between capabilities and costs, and appropriate estimating methodologies selected. It requires an extensive database of the costs of existing equipment and personnel.

The cost methodology results in separate estimates for the network infrastructure and the other resources required for a military operation. These are summed to provide the total life-cycle cost of networked operations. The methodology links network capabilities to cost so that decisionmakers are aware of how capabilities drive costs. It allows an assessment of the total cost and affordability of performing different operations, with and without networks. It also allows costs and benefits to be calculated for each operation.

6. Conclusion

As Sweden makes major decisions regarding its future security strategy, the extent and nature of the military's network options will become clearer. Meanwhile, this report and similar work can help build a better understanding of many of the issues associated with creating a modern military network.

This report has been intended to assist the Swedish Armed Forces and their supporting agencies gain a clearer understanding of network-based operations and many of the issues associated with creating a complex series of interrelated military networks. It has provided terminology and concepts associated with military networking as part of developing a common reference for discussing network-based operations, which will be important as the military moves increasingly in the direction of this new way of commanding, controlling, and executing military operations.

Additionally, the study highlighted sample functions that could be included in a series of military networks, including those that would have applicability in normal peacetime operations, as well as during an actual military operation. Other functions are more directly related to actual operations. The major defence policy decisions that Sweden will make in the coming years will help guide the prioritisation of these functions. Fiscal and technology realities will mean that networking will gradually enter the Swedish military, so introducing first those functions that relate to the types of operations the Swedish military is most likely to undertake must be given highest priority.

The costing of military networks is still an imprecise art, much less a science. Since the concept of networked-based operations is still being introduced into the better militaries of the world, there are few lessons and past experiences that provide guidance on how to approach costing of new systems. The report provided insights on what are likely to be major cost drivers in military networks. One of the most critical, and most difficult to predict, of such drivers is software development. Past experience in major military projects indicates that software development times and costs can be difficult to forecast accurately. Since the Swedish military is still developing its concepts of network-based operations, early definition of requirements can help in such forecasting, as can an awareness of the major issues associated with network-development costs. Those issues have been highlighted in this report.

This report is part of the initial effort to move the Swedish Armed Forces into the realm of high-performance military network-based operations. The nation's military is firmly committed to this fascinating new area, which should result in significantly enhanced capabilities. Much additional research must be done in an operational, conceptual, and technological sense. Next steps beyond this report could include the examination of how different network options could enhance the performance of the Swedish military in various hypothetical missions, ranging from high-intensity combat down to peace support operations. The upcoming defence policy decisions will help to prioritise the networking research. Meanwhile, various options can be explored in order to develop a better understanding of how networks can function, their operational utility, the technical issues involved, and the costs associated with different levels of network complexity and functionality.

Appendix

Measurement Categories

In Chapter 3, we used the Conceptual Framework for NCW (Signori et al., 2002) as the basis for the capabilities and measures. This framework is designed to be tailored to specific applications, such as the evaluation of networks discussed in this document. In the process of conducting this tailoring, we changed some of the terminology to avoid confusion. Changes to the capabilities are summarised in Table A.1; changes to the measures are summarised in Table A.2.

Table A.1

Terminology Correlations—Capabilities

A Conceptual Framework for NCW	New Terminology	Justification
Interactions	Collaboration	*Interactions* is intended to generalise from *collaboration*, or deliberate, purposeful interactions, to include all social or socio-technical interactions. For the purpose of evaluating a network, we are primarily interested in support for deliberate interactions, so we retain the term *collaboration* to avoid confusion with the interaction categories.
Information Share-ability	Discovery and Collection	Discovery and collection is a subset of information shareability that focuses on retrieval of information.
Networking	Network Connectivity Network Control	Networking has been considered as two capabilities—network connectivity and network control—because we wish to distinguish between the infrastructure (connectivity) aspects and the operational (control) aspects of network performance.

Table A.2

Terminology Correlations—Measures

A Conceptual Framework for NCW	New Terminology	Justification
Intensity	Collaboration Intensity Collaboration Timeliness	*Intensity* includes both the variety of communications modes and timeliness concerns. Because these correspond to different axes of complexity in Figure 3.1, they have been separated.
Agility	Collaboration Robustness Connectivity Robustness Capacity Control Access Control	Robustness and adaptability (control) are two submeasures of agility, which also includes responsiveness, flexibility, and innovativeness.
Assurance	Network Link Security Node Security Data Security	The term *security* is consistent with the axes of interaction and makes it explicit that robustness is covered separately.
Ease of Use Quantity of Retrieved Information	Organisation Navigation Storage Capacity Data Timeliness	These metrics are all associated with information shareability. However, while the NCW conceptual framework metrics capture the *ease* of *presentation* (ease of use) and the *quantity* of *retrieved* information, organisation and navigation capture the *ease* of *retrieving* information. Data timeliness and storage capacity are also related to the retrieval and storage of information. Note that the NCW conceptual framework also includes a similar attribute: timeliness of individual information.
Information Postage Information Retrieval	Information Reach	This is a measure that is independent of personnel.
Quality of Service	Connectivity Capacity Bandwidth control Monitoring Security	These are submeasures.
	Access time	This is an additional submeasure of net-ready nodes that is not captured in the NCW Conceptual Framework.

Table A.2—Continued

A Conceptual Framework for NCW	New Terminology	Justification
Posting and Retrieval Capability Support	Information Accessibility	This shorter term is preferred as it is a more common and easily understood term, although its link to posting and retrieval capability support is given in the text.
Connectivity	Node Connectivity	This distinguishes the term from network connectivity.

Bibliography

Alberts, D. S., *Information Age Transformation: Getting to a 21st Century Military*, rev. ed., Washington, D.C.: Command and Control Research Program (CCRP), 2002.

Alberts, D. S., Gartska, J., and Stein, F., *Network Centric Warfare*, 2nd ed. (rev.), Washington, D.C.: CCRP, 2000.

Assistant Secretary of Defense for Command Control Communications and Intelligence and the U.S. Joint Staff (J-6, Communications), *C4ISR Architecture Working Group Final Report*, April 14, 1998. Available at http://www.fas.org/irp/program/core/fnlrprt.pdf. Last accessed December 23, 2003.

Barnett, T., "The Seven Deadly Sins of Network-Centric Warfare," *Proceedings, U.S. Naval Institute*, 1999.

Boehm, B., et al., "Cost Models for Future Software Life Cycle Processes: COCOMO 2.0," in J. D. Arthur and S. M. Henry, eds., *Annals of Software Engineering, Special Volume on Software Process and Product Measurement*, Amsterdam, The Netherlands: J. C. Baltzer AG, Science Publishers, 1995.

Cebrowski, A., and Gartska, J., "Network-Centric Warfare—Its Origin and Future," *Proceedings, U.S. Naval Institute*, Vol. 124/1/1139, January 1998, pp. 28–35.

Clark, Thea, and Richard Jones, "Organisational Interoperability Maturity Model for C2," *Proceedings of the 1999 Command and Control Research and Technology Symposium*, Newport, R.I., June 1999.

Clark, T., and Moon, T., "Interoperability for Joint and Coalition Operations," *Australian Defence Journal*, No. 151, November/December 2001, pp. 23–36.

Congressional Research Service, *Navy Network-Centric Warfare Concept: Key Programs and Issues for Congress*, Washington, D.C.: The Library of Congress, January 30, 2002.

"The Cooperative Engagement Capability," *Johns Hopkins Technical Digest*, Vol. 16, No. 4, 1995.

Department of the Navy, *Fiscal Year 2004/2005 Biennial Budget Estimates, Justification of Estimates, February 2003, Research, Development, Test and Evaluation, Navy, Budget Activity 4*, 2003.

Dunn, Beth, *Introduction to Cost Analysis*, Washington, D.C.: Defence Acquisition University, Business, Cost Estimating, and Financial Management Department, October 2002. Available at http://center.dau.mil/Topical_Sessions templates/FM1/template.htm. Last accessed December 23, 2003.

European Institute, "Transatlantic Interoperability in Defence Industries," Washington, D.C., 2002.

European Union, "WEU Council of Ministers Petersberg Declaration," Bonn, June 19, 1992. Available at http://www.cip.fuhem.es/ueh/ documentos/ueo/92-petersberg.htm. Last accessed December 23, 2003.

Grant, C., "CEC: Sensor Netting with Integrated Fire Control," *Johns Hopkins APL Technical Digest*, Vol. 23, Nos. 2 and 3, 2002, pp. 149–161.

Jones, C., "Sizing Up Software," *Scientific American*, Vol. 279, No. 6, 1998, pp. 104–109.

Li, A., and Brook, J. L., Jr., *Observations on the Procurement of the Navy/Marine Corps Intranet, Statement for the Record by Allen Li, Associate Director, Defense Acquisitions Issues, National Security and International Affairs Division, and Jack L. Brook, Jr., Director, Governmentwide and Defense Information Systems, Accounting and Information Management Division, United States General Accounting Office,* GAO Testimony Before the Subcommittees on Military Readiness and Military Research and Development, Committee on Armed Services, House of Representatives, Washington, D.C., GAO/T-NSIAD/AIMD-00-116, for release March 8, 2000.

Ministry of Defence, *Budget Bill 2002*, Stockholm, September 2001a.

Ministry of Defence, *Budget Bill 2002 Fact Sheet*, Stockholm, presented to Parliament on 20 September 2001b.

Ministry of Defence, *Cooperation Within the EU, Stockholm*, February 2002.

Ministry of Defence, *The New Defence—Prepared for the Next Millennium*, Stockholm: Swedish Defence Policy Paper, A short version of the Government Bill, 1999/2000.

NATO, "NATO Fact Sheet: Partnership and Cooperation," NATO On-line Library, February, 2002. Available at http://www.nato.int/docu/ facts/2001/part-coop.htm. Last accessed December 23, 2003.

NATO, "NATO Glossary of Terms and Definitions", NATO On-line Library, AAP-6, December 19, 2003. Available at http://www.nato.int/docu/ stanag/aap006/aap6.htm. Last accessed December 23, 2003.

"NATO: A List of Signatures of the Partnership for Peace Framework Document," NATO On-line Library, April 23, 2003. Available at http://www.nato.int/pfp/sig-cntr.htm. Last accessed December 23, 2003.

"The Network Is the Battlefield," Special Report: Military Technology, *Business Week*, January 7, 2003.

PerP Rapport 7, Draft FOI briefing, personal communication, remiss 1, December 2002.

Perry, Walt, et al., "Advanced Metrics for Network-Centric Naval Operations," Santa Monica, Calif.: unpublished RAND Corporation research.

Perry, Walt, Robert W. Button, Jerome Bracken, Thomas J. Sullivan, and Jonathan Mitchell, *Measures of Effectiveness for the Information-Age Navy: The Effects of Network-Centric Operations on Combat Outcomes*, Santa Monica, Calif.: RAND Corporation, MR-1449-NAVY, 2001.

Pfleeger, Shari Lawrence, *Software Engineering Theory and Practice,* 2nd ed., Upper Saddle River, N.J.: Prentice-Hall, 2001.

"Revolution in Military Affairs—the Swedish Programme," *Swedish Journal of Military Technology,* Vol. 3, 2000, p. 6.

Signori, D., Alberts, D., and Hayes, R., "A Conceptual Framework for Network Centric Warfare," *NCW/NEC Workshop*, Held at Evidence Based Research Incorporated, McLean Va., December 2002. Only available online at http://www.dodccrp.org/ncw_workshop/IntroductoryBriefs/SignoriAConceptualFrameworkforNCW.ppt. Last accessed December 23, 2003.

The Standish Group, *The Chaos Report*, 1994. Available at http://www.standishgroup.com/sample_research/chaos_1994_1.php. Last accessed December 23, 2003.

Stein, F. P., "Observations on the Emergence of Network-Centric Warfare." Available at www.dodccrp.org/steincw.htm.

"Sweden Stands Committed to Network-Centric Warfare," *Defense News*, March 18–24, 2002, p. 10.

"Sweden, U.S. in Trade Deal," *Defense News*, January 28–February 3, 2002, p. 1.

Verton, Dan, "Huge Navy IT Outsourcing Deal Passes First Hurdle, Multibillion-dollar Navy/Marine Corps, Intranet Given OK, but Challenges Remain," *Computerworld*, May 13, 2002.

Younossi, Obaid, Mark V. Arena, Richard M. Moore, Mark A. Lorell, Joanna Mason, and John C. Graser, *Military Jet Engine Acquisition: Technology Basics and Cost-Estimating Methodology*, Santa Monica, Calif.: RAND Corporation, MR-1596-AF, 2002.